eorge F. Kennan

American Diplomacy

Expanded Edition

American Diplomacy

American Diplomacy

EXPANDED EDITION

GEORGE F. KENNAN

THE UNIVERSITY OF CHICAGO PRESS

CHICAGO AND LONDON

Burgess
E
744
K3
1984

The University of Chicago Press, Chicago 60637
The University of Chicago Press, Ltd., London

© 1951, 1979 by The University of Chicago
© 1984 by George F. Kennan
All rights reserved. Published 1951
College edition 1969. Paper edition 1970
Expanded edition 1984
Printed in the United States of America

93 92 91 90 89 88 87 86 85 84   5 4 3 2 1

Library of Congress Cataloging in Publication Data

Kennan, George Frost, 1904–
  American diplomacy.

  Rev. ed. of: American diplomacy, 1900–1950. 1951.
  1. United States—Foreign relations—20th century—
Addresses, essays, lectures. 2. United States—Foreign
relations—Soviet Union—Addresses, essays, lectures.
3. Soviet Union—Foreign relations—United States—
Addresses, essays, lectures. I. Kennan, George Frost,
1904–   . American diplomacy, 1900–1950. II. Title.
E744.K3 1984   327.73   84–24085
ISBN 0–226–43146–0 (cloth)
ISBN 0–226–43147–9 (paper)

TABLE OF CONTENTS

✿

FOREWORD, 1985

✵

WHEN there came to me, in the winter of 1950, an invitation to deliver a series of lectures at the University of Chicago, I had no idea what academic lecturing really was. I had visions of a series of informal discourses in small groups, and I thought this might give me an opportunity (as indeed it finally did) to bring to bear on certain of the problems of American diplomacy a few of the insights induced by a quarter of a century of practical diplomatic experience. The occasion proved to be a far greater challenge than I had expected. Not only was this true in the immediate sense (of student attention), but it was even more true from the standpoint of the enduring attention the lectures were to continue to receive over the ensuing decades. This last is the justification for their re-publication today in an expanded form.

I emphasize the phrase "in an expanded form," because the two final lectures, delivered only recently at Grinnell College, and added to this volume as Part III, are included here for a purpose. They treat, at least in part, of questions which have since come to preoccupy American opinion but which were not, and indeed could not be, treated in 1950. Outstanding among those questions were the ones evoked by the nuclear weapons race and those that arose in connection with the emergence of the Cold War during and after the conflict in Korea.

The problem of nuclear weaponry was not treated in the Chicago lectures because I still continued at that time to hope, naively if you will, that we would pause before entering the chamber of horrors that I saw looming before us in any decision to base our defenses on weapons of this nature and to encourage others to do likewise. I would have liked to see the "atomic bomb" (as it was then called) rejected, as a device too terrible and too indiscriminate to constitute a useful weapon, and ignored accordingly. So far as our policy on nuclear weapons was considered, the score was not yet in. I did not want to encourage speculation on this subject. It was best, I thought, to try to help people find answers to our problems in a non-nuclear environment. This was hard enough in itself. And as far as the political aspects of the Cold War were concerned, the Korean War was on, to be sure; but it was new. Its outcome was still in doubt, as was our policy with relation to it. Its lessons were not yet fully apparent, and the post-Stalin era was not yet visible.

So what I talked about, there at Chicago, was American diplomacy of the first half of this century, in its familiar pre-nuclear and pre-1945 environment. Only the final lecture went as far as World War II; and that lecture dwelt only on the origins of that war and on the interpretation of its historical significance, not on its consequences.

As for the two documents that form Part II of this text (both articles written for *Foreign Affairs*), they were appended to the original published version of the Chicago lectures. One of them was written at a much earlier date, when the outlines of postwar problems were even less visible; the other, written almost simultaneously with the Chicago lectures, was subject to the same restraints as the ones delivered at Chicago.

The Grinnell lectures were intended to cover only a small part of the resulting gap and to deal only with limited aspects of the specific, and in many ways new, problems that have assailed American policymakers in the years since 1950. Yet certain of these aspects—particularly those concerning problems we faced in the Far East—have a special relationship to the ones treated at Chicago, and it therefore seems suitable to include them in this volume.

The problems of excessive legalism and moralism, as treated in the original lectures, are today, in large part, historical ones. To be sure, we still have a tendency to fall back on both of these extremes when it suits our purpose to do so. But the bewilderments of the Cold War have produced strange consequences, and there are times in these recent years when I have found myself wishing that there were a bit more of morality in our concepts of what is legal, and more attention to legality in our concepts of what is moral, than I see around me at this time. Perhaps our diplomacy of the first five decades of this century, and our reactions to the very different problems that have assailed us since 1950, both reflect realities much deeper than our specific responses of either period: namely, the lack of any accepted, enduring

doctrine for relating military strength to political policy, and a persistent tendency to fashion our policy towards others with a view to feeding a pleasing image of ourselves rather than to achieving real, and
desperately needed, results in our relations with others. Perhaps this
book will serve a purpose in bringing both these deficiencies to our
national consciousness.

George Kennan

FOREWORD

✿

AFTER many years of official duty in the Foreign Service of
the United States, it fell to me to bear a share of the responsibility for forming the foreign policy of the United
States in the difficult years following World War II. The Policy
Planning Staff—it was my duty to set up this office and direct
it through the first years of its existence—was the first regular
office of the Department of State to be charged in our time
with looking at problems from the standpoint of the totality
of American national interest, as distinct from a single portion
of it. People working in this institutional framework soon became conscious of the lack of any general agreement, both
within and without our government, on the basic concepts
underlying the conduct of the external relations of the United
States.

It was this realization of the lack of an adequately stated
and widely accepted theoretical foundation to underpin the
conduct of our external relations which aroused my curiosity
about the concepts by which our statesmen had been guided in
recent decades. After all, the novel and grave problems with
which we were forced to deal seemed in large measure to be
the products of the outcome of these past two world wars.
The rhythm of international events is such that the turn of the
century seemed a suitable starting point for an examination
of American diplomacy and its relation to these two great
cycles of violence. One and a half decades elapsed between the
conclusion of the war with Spain and the dispatch of the first
"Open Door" notes, on the one hand, and the outbreak of
World War I, on the other. Measured against what we know

of the relationships between cause and effect in the great matters of international life, this is a respectable period of time
and one in which the influence of a country as powerful as the
United States of that day could, if exerted consistently and
with determination, have affected perceptibly the course of
world affairs. The same was plainly true of the interval between the two world wars. By 1900 we were generally aware
that our power had world-wide significance and that we could
be affected by events far afield; from that time on our interests were constantly involved in important ways with such
events.

By what concepts were our statesmen animated in their
efforts to meet these new problems? What assumptions had
they made concerning the basic purposes of this country in the
field of foreign policy? What was it they felt they were trying
to achieve? And were these concepts, in the light of retrospect,
appropriate and effective ones? Did they reflect some deeper
understanding of the relationship of American democracy to
its world environment—something which we, perhaps, had
forgotten but ought to resurrect and place again at the foundation of our conduct? Or had they been inadequate and superficial all along?

It was these questions which drew my curiosity to the
record of America's diplomatic activity in this past half-century, a record which has become steadily richer with the continued appearance of private memoirs and papers and the excellent efforts of American scholarship in the study and analysis of this material. As a novice in the field of diplomatic history, I could not hope to contribute to this work of research
or even to make a comprehensive examination of all the secondary material which has appeared on these subjects. The lectures included in this volume, therefore, represent only an attempt to apply what might be called a layman's reading of the
main published materials—fortified by the curiosity described

above—to the questions at hand and to indicate the answers that suggested themselves.

Two somewhat contradictory considerations gave to this inquiry a special edge of interest from my own standpoint. The first of these was the recognition that the formulation of American foreign policy from the time of the Spanish-American War until the end of World War II had absorbed the energies and contributions of a number of outstanding Americans —men of exceptional intelligence and education, deeply respected for their integrity of character and breadth of experience. In certain instances, they were substantially the best we had to offer. If their approaches to the philosophy of external relations were inadequate, then the deficiencies of America's understanding of her own relationship to the rest of the globe, and her interest in shaping this relationship, were deeply rooted in the national consciousness, and any corrections would be difficult indeed.

Coupled with this, one had the inescapable fact that our security, or what we took to be our security, had suffered a tremendous decline over the course of the half-century. A country which in 1900 had no thought that its prosperity and way of life could be in any way threatened by the outside world had arrived by 1950 at a point where it seemed to be able to think of little else but this danger.

What was the explanation for this? To what extent was it the fault of American diplomacy? To the extent that it *was* the fault of American diplomacy, what was wrong—the concepts or the execution? To the extent that it might be the result of things outside the range of our influence, what were these things and what did they portend? Were they still operable, and where would they carry us? There could be no thought of answering these questions exhaustively in six lectures, even had one felt that he had the answers. The lectures in this volume, then, constitute attempts to discuss individual episodes and situations in the light of these questions, in the hope that this impressionistic pattern may communicate better than any attempt at direct presentation my own reactions to the material at hand. Only in the last of them is there any effort at generalization. I am sure they will be vulnerable in matters of detail to the critical judgment of the experienced diplomatic historian. The conclusions they indicate will certainly be widely challenged. If they serve as a stimulus to further thought on these problems and to worthier efforts by wiser and more learned people, their purpose will be served.

The lectures given at the University of Chicago, embracing as they did American diplomacy up to and through World War II, had little direct reference to the problems of Soviet-American relations, which have agitated so deeply the public opinion of our day. For this reason, it may not be easy for everyone to discern the full measure of their relevance to current problems. It was thought appropriate, therefore, to include in this volume two articles on Russian-American relations which can be taken as reflecting the application of the same intellectual approach to problems of the present day.

I acknowledge here my gratitude to the officers of the Charles R. Walgreen Foundation for the Study of American Institutions, which sponsored these six lectures, and to the Editor of *Foreign Affairs*, in which the two articles were originally published.

GEORGE F. KENNAN

PRINCETON, NEW JERSEY

PART I

I

THE WAR WITH SPAIN

✣

I WOULD like first to say a word about the concept of these six lectures. This concept stems from no abstract interest in history for history's sake. It stems from a preoccupation with the problems of foreign policy we have before us today.

A half-century ago people in this country had a sense of security vis-à-vis their world environment such as I suppose no people had ever had since the days of the Roman Empire. Today that pattern is almost reversed—our national consciousness is dominated at present by a sense of insecurity greater even than that of many of the peoples of western Europe who stand closer to, and in a position far more vulnerable to, those things that are the main source of our concern. Now, much of that change may be, and doubtless is, subjective—a reflection of the fact that in 1900 we exaggerated the security of our position and had an overweening confidence in our strength and our ability to solve problems, whereas today we exaggerate our dangers and have a tendency to rate our own abilities less than they actually are. But the fact remains that much of this change is also objectively real; in 1900 the political and military realities were truly such that we had relatively little to fear in the immediate sense, whereas today we have before us a situation which, I am frank to admit, seems to me dangerous and problematical in the extreme.

What has caused this metamorphosis? How did a country so secure become a country so insecure? How much of this deterioration can be said to be "our fault"? How much of it is attributable to our failure to see clearly, or to take into account, the realities of the world around us?

What lessons, in other words, does the record of the external relations of the United States over the last fifty years hold for us, the generation of 1951, pressed and hemmed in as we are by a thousand troubles and dangers, surrounded by a world part of which seems to be actually committed to our destruction and another part to have lost confidence either in ourselves or in itself, or in both?

These are the questions which have taken me back, in the past few months, to a review of some of our decisions of national policy in these fifty years. I certainly cannot hold out to you the hope that this series of lectures will answer all these questions, or will answer any one of them in a manner beyond controversy.

But what we can hope, I think, is that it will be useful to turn again to certain of the major phases of national policy over this period and to look at them once more in the light of what seem in retrospect to have been their alternatives and their consequences. We have good reason for doing this. Not only is there much that should be visible to us now that was not visible to people as little as ten years ago; but I would hope that we might bring to such an inquiry a new sort of seriousness—a seriousness induced by our recollection of the vast destruction and the sacrifices we have witnessed in our lifetimes, a seriousness more thoughtful and sadder than most people would have been able to bring to these problems in the days before the two tragic world wars.

What I would like to talk about first is the Spanish-American War.

Today, standing at the end rather than the beginning of this half-century, some of us see certain fundamental elements on which we suspect that American security has rested. We can see that our security has been dependent throughout much of our history on the position of Britain; that Canada, in particular, has been a useful and indispensable hostage to good relations between our country and the British Empire; and that Britain's position, in turn, has depended on the maintenance of a balance of power on the European Continent. Thus it was essential to us, as it was to Britain, that no single Continental land power should come to dominate the entire Eurasian land mass. Our interest has lain rather in the maintenance of some sort of stable balance among the powers of the interior, in order that none of them should effect the subjugation of the others, conquer the seafaring fringes of the land mass, become a great sea power as well as land power, shatter the position of England, and enter—as in these circumstances it certainly would—on an overseas expansion hostile to ourselves and supported by the immense resources of the interior of Europe and Asia. Seeing these things, we can understand that we have had a stake in the prosperity and independence of the peripheral powers of Europe and Asia: those countries whose gazes were oriented outward, across the seas, rather than inward to the conquest of power on land.

Now we see these things, or think we see them. But they were scarcely yet visible to the Americans of 1898, for those Americans had forgotten a great deal that had been known to their forefathers of a hundred years before. They had become so accustomed to their security that they had forgotten that it had any foundations at all outside our continent. They mistook our sheltered position behind the British fleet and British Continental diplomacy for the results of superior American wisdom and virtue in refraining from interfering in the sordid differences of the Old World. And they were oblivious to the first portents of the changes that were destined to shatter that pattern of security in the course of the ensuing half-century.

There were, of course, exceptions. Brooks Adams, Henry's brother, probably came closer than any American of his day to a sort of an intellectual premonition of what the future had in store for us.[1] But even he caught only a portion of it. He saw the increasing vulnerability of England—the increasing "eccentricity," as he called it, of her economic position, her growing economic dependence on the United States—and, conversely, the growing strategic dependence of the United States on England. He sensed the ultimate importance of the distinction between sea power and land power. Vaguely, he felt the danger of political collaboration between Russia and Germany and China. But his thinking was distorted by the materialism of the time: by the overestimation of economics, of trade, as factors in human events and by the corresponding underestimation of psychological and political reactions—of such things as fear, ambition, insecurity, jealousy, and perhaps even boredom—as prime movers of events.

Mahan, too, was charting new paths at that time in the analysis of international realities—paths which led in the direction of a more profound appraisal of the sources of American security. And there were others who might be mentioned. But altogether they comprised only a tiny coterie of persons. Their efforts were not even followed up by others at the time or in the years that immediately ensued. Those efforts remained suspended, as it were, in the mid-air of history—an isolated spurt of intellectual activity against a background of general torpor and smugness in American thinking about foreign affairs. And all of them—all of these deeper and more observant minds of the turn of the century—stopped short of the projection of their inquiry onto the theater of European Continental rivalries where, as it happened, the events most fateful to American security were destined to occur and where we stood in the greatest need of profound analysis and careful identification of the elements of American interest.

1. "The Spanish War and the Equilibrium of the World," in *America's Economic Supremacy*, by Brooks Adams. New edition with evaluation by Marquis W. Childs (New York, 1947).

It is plain, for this reason, that the incident I am talking about today—our brief war with Spain in 1898—occurred against a background of public and governmental thinking in this country which was not marked by any great awareness of the global framework of our security. This being the case, it was fortunate that both the situation out of which the war arose and, for the most part, the events and consequences of the war itself were largely local and domestic in their importance. As we proceed with these lectures and advance into the twentieth century, we shall see the global implications of our predicaments and actions growing apace with the passage of the years, until in the case of World War II they are positively overwhelming. But at the time of the Spanish-American War they were hardly present at all—the taking of the Philippines was the closest we came to them. And if a war so colorless from the standpoint of our world relationships is worth discussing at all this afternoon, it is because it forms a sort of preface to our examination of the diplomacy of this half-century, a simple, almost quaint, illustration of some of our national reactions and ways of doing business, and a revelation of the distance we were destined to have to come if we were ever to be a power capable of coping with the responsibilities of world leadership.

Our war with Spain, as you will recall, grew out of a situation in Cuba. It was one of those dreadful, tragic, hopeless situations which seem to mark the decline or exhaustion of a colonial relationship. We have seen other such situations since, and some of them not so long ago. Spanish rule on the island was challenged by Cuban insurgents, poorly organized, poorly disciplined, but operating on the classical principles of guerrilla forces everywhere and enjoying all the advantages of guerrillas operating on the home territory against an unpopular foreign enemy. The Spanish attempts to suppress the insurrection were inefficient, cruel, and only partly successful. The situation had been long developing; it had been growing sporadically for decades. President Grant had summed it up very well in a presidential message, over two decades earlier, in 1875:

Each party seems quite capable of working great injury and damage to the other, as well as to all the relations and interests dependent on the existence of peace in the island; but they seem incapable of reaching any adjustment, and both have thus far failed of achieving any success whereby one party shall possess and control the island to the exclusion of the other. Under these circumstances, the agency of others, either by mediation or intervention, seems to be the only alternative which must sooner or later be invoked for the termination of the strife.[2]

There had been some improvement, to be sure, in the two decades between 1875 and 1895. But in that latter year insurrection broke out again, this time on a bloodier and more tragic scale than ever before. And in the years 1896 and 1897 it brought increasing concern and dismay to the government, the press, and the public in our country.

Strictly speaking, of course, it would have been possible for us to have said that it was none of our business and to have let things take their course. Our national security, as we think of it today, was not threatened. But American property interests were damaged; the activities of American filibusterers and arms salesmen, on behalf of the insurgents, caused a lot of trouble to our government. And, above all, American public opinion was deeply shocked by the tales of violence and misery from the island. Our sensibilities were not yet jaded by the immense horrors and cruelties of the twentieth century. The sufferings of the Cuban people shocked our sensibilities, aroused our indignation. They gave American statesmen the conviction that a continuation of this situation in Cuba would be intolerable to our interests in the long run and that, if Spain did not succeed in putting an end to it, we should have to intervene in some way ourselves.

2. Message of the President, December 7, 1875.

In the fall of 1897 things looked up a bit. A new and more moderate government came into power in Spain. This government showed a greater disposition to clear up the unhappy problems on the island than had its predecessor. In his message to Congress in December, 1897, President McKinley noted this improvement and recommended that we give the new Spanish government a chance. "I shall not impugn its sincerity," he said, "nor should impatience be suffered to embarrass it in the task it has undertaken." Certain difficulties, he said, had already been cleared up; there was reason to hope that, with patience on our part and continued good will on the part of the Spanish government, further progress might be made. Thus the year 1898 began with a renewed hope that the plight of the Cuban people might get better instead of worse.

Unfortunately, two things happened during the winter which changed the situation quite drastically. First, the Spanish minister in Washington wrote an indiscreet letter in which he spoke slightingly of President McKinley, calling him "a bidder for the admiration of the crowd" and "a would-be politician . . . who tries to leave a door open behind himself while keeping on good terms with the jingoes of his party."[3] This letter leaked; it was published in the New York papers, causing much indignation and resentment. And a few days later the American public was profoundly shocked and outraged to hear that the battleship "Maine" had been sunk in Havana harbor with the loss of 266 American lives.

Now, looked at in retrospect, neither of these incidents seems to have been an adequate cause, in itself, for war. The Spanish government could not help its minister's indiscretion—even diplomats are constantly being indiscreet, this sort of thing happens in the best of families. It promptly removed him from his job and disavowed his offensive state-

3. Letter from Dupuy de Lome quoted by Charles S. Olcott in *William McKinley* (Boston and New York, 1916), II, 9.

ments. And, as for the "Maine," there has never been any evidence that the Spanish government had anything to do with the sinking of the vessel or would have been anything but horrified at the suggestion that it should have anything to do with it. Spanish authorities, as well as our own consul-general in Havana, had begged us not to send the vessel there at that time for the very reason that they were afraid this might lead to trouble. The Spanish government did everything in its power to mitigate the effects of the catastrophe, welcomed investigation, and eventually offered to submit the whole question of responsibility to international arbitration—an offer we never accepted.

Nevertheless, it seems to be the judgment of history that these two incidents so affected American opinion that war became inevitable with the sinking of the "Maine." From that time on no peaceful solution was really given serious consideration in the American government. This is particularly significant and unfortunate, because during the nine weeks that intervened between the sinking of the "Maine" and the opening of hostilities the Spanish government came very far in the direction of meeting our demands and desires. It came so far that by April 10 (eleven days before hostilities began) our minister in Madrid—a wise and moderate man who had worked hard to prevent the outbreak of war—was able to report that, if the President could get from Congress authority to deal with the matter at his own discretion, he could have a final settlement before August 1 on one of the following bases: autonomy acceptable to the insurgents, independence, or cession to the United States. On the same day, the queen of Spain ordered a complete armistice on the island, and the Spanish minister in Washington promised to our government the early promulgation of a system of autonomy "such that no motive or pretext is left for claiming any fuller measure thereof."[4]

4. *Foreign Relations of the United States, 1898* (Washington, 1901), p. 747.

These are of course isolated snatches out of a long and involved correspondence between the two governments. I cite them only to indicate that on paper, at least, the Spanish government was coming around very rapidly in those early days of April, 1898, to the sort of attitude and action we had been demanding of them. Yet, despite all that, one finds no evidence that the United States government was in any way influenced by these last-minute concessions. It made no move to prevent feeling and action in Congress from proceeding along a line that was plainly directed toward an early outbreak of hostilities.

Now, it is true that, as people then saw it, many of these Spanish concessions came too late and were not fully dependable. It is also true that the insurgents were by this time in no frame of mind, and in no state of discipline, to collaborate in any way with the Spanish authorities. But one does not get the impression that these were the things which dictated the decision of our government to go to war. This decision seems rather attributable to the state of American opinion, to the fact that it was a year of congressional elections, to the unabashed and really fantastic warmongering of a section of the American press, and to the political pressures which were freely and bluntly exerted on the President from various political quarters. (It is an interesting fact, incidentally, that financial and business circles, allegedly the instigators of wars, had no part in this and generally frowned on the idea of our involvement in the hostilities.)

The upshot of all this, as you know, was that on April 20 Congress resolved that "it is the duty of the United States to demand, and the Government of the United States does hereby demand, that the Government of Spain at once relinquish its authority and government in the island of Cuba and withdraw its land and naval forces from Cuba and Cuban waters." And it directed and empowered the President "to use the entire land

and naval forces of the United States . . . to such extent as may be necessary" to enforce that requirement. We gave the Spaniards a flat three-day ultimatum for compliance with this resolution. We knew they would not, and could not, accept it. Early the following morning the Spaniards, without waiting for the delivery of the ultimatum, declared the resolution "equivalent to a declaration of war" and broke relations. On the same day, hostilities were inaugurated by the United States government. Thus our government, to the accompaniment of great congressional and popular acclaim, inaugurated hostilities against another country in a situation of which it can only be said that the possibilities of settlement by measures short of war had by no means been exhausted.

So much for the origin of the war. Now a few words about the way we fought it and particularly about the taking of the Philippines. You will recall that the wording of the congressional resolution which I just quoted mentioned only the island of Cuba. There was nothing in the resolution to indicate that Congress had any interest in any territory other than Cuba or that the President was authorized to use the armed forces for any purpose not directly related to the Spanish withdrawal from Cuba. Now, this resolution was passed on April 20, 1898. Yet it was only eleven days later that Admiral Dewey, sailing into Manila Bay in the early hours of morning, attacked and destroyed the Spanish fleet there. And only a few days later President McKinley authorized preparations for the dispatch of an army of occupation. The mission of this ground force was to follow up Dewey's victory, to complete "the reduction of Spanish power in that quarter," and to give "order and security to the islands while in the possession of the United States."[5] This force proceeded to the Philippines and went into action there. By August it stormed and took the city of Manila. The effect of this action was later to constitute

5. Olcott, *op. cit.*, II, 166–67.

the most important and probably decisive consideration in our final decision to take the islands away from Spain and put them under the United States flag entirely; for this military operation shattered Spanish rule in the islands, made it impossible for us to leave them to Spain, and left us, as we shall see shortly, no agreeable alternative but to take them ourselves.

Now, why did all this happen? If there was no justification for the action against the Philippines in the origin of the war with Spain, what were the motives that lay behind it? Why, in other words, did we do things in May, 1898, that made it almost impossible for us later not to annex a great archipelago in the South Seas in which, prior to this time, our interest had been virtually nil? I ask this question not as one of moral judgment of American statesmen of the time but as one which may illumine the ways by which decisions are taken, and business done, by the United States government.

The fact of the matter is that down to the present day we do not know the full answer to this question. We know a number of things about it. We know that Theodore Roosevelt, who was then the young Assistant Secretary of the Navy, had long felt that we ought to take the Philippines; that he wangled Dewey's appointment to the command of the Asiatic fleet; that both he and Dewey wanted war; and that he had some sort of a prior understanding with Dewey to the effect that Dewey would attack Manila, regardless of the circumstances of the origin or the purpose of the war. We know that President McKinley, in defending Dewey's action at a later date, showed a very poor understanding of what was really involved and professed to believe a number of strategic premises that simply were not true. McKinley indicated that he had no thought of taking the Philippines at the time of the Battle of Manila and that Dewey's action was designed only to destroy the Spanish fleet and eliminate it as a factor in the war. But, if this is true, we are still mystified as to why McKinley author-ized the sending of any army of occupation to the islands with-in a few days of Dewey's victory. We are not sure that we really know what passed between the government in Washing-ton and Dewey prior to the battle. And we can only say that it looks very much as though, in this case, the action of the United States government had been determined primarily on the basis of a very able and quiet intrigue by a few strategi-cally placed persons in Washington, an intrigue which re-ceived absolution, forgiveness, and a sort of a public blessing by virtue of war hysteria—of the fact that Dewey's victory was so thrilling and pleasing to the American public—but which, had its results been otherwise, might well have found its ending in the rigors of a severe and extremely unpleasant congressional investigation.

So much, then, for the decisions underlying our conduct of hostilities. What about the broader political decisions con-nected with the war—the decisions which led to the final an-nexation not only of the Philippines but of Puerto Rico and Guam and the Hawaiian Islands? These were very important decisions from our own standpoint. They represented a turning point, it seems to me, in the whole concept of the American political system. These territorial acquisitions of the year 1898 represented the first extensions of United States sovereignty to important territories beyond the continental limits of North America, unless our share in the ruling of Samoa warranted such description. They represented the first instances of sizable populations being taken under our flag with no wide anticipa-tion that they would ever be accepted into statehood. Prior to this time our territorial acquisitions had been relatively empty lands, too sparsely populated to be eligible at once for state-hood. For them the territorial status was viewed as a tem-porary expedient, intended to tide them over until they were filled with our own sort of people and were prepared to come into the Union.

But here, in 1898, for the first time, territories were acquired which were not expected to gain statehood at all at any time but rather to remain indefinitely in a status of colonial subordination. The leading advocates of expansion were quite definite on this point. One of the most thoughtful and articulate of them, Whitelaw Reid, often expressed his anxiety lest people might think of the new territories as candidates for statehood, because he knew that, if they did, they would be less inclined to take them in. Andrew Carnegie, who was an opponent of expansionism, attacked Reid on precisely this point: "You will be driven off from your opposition to letting all these islands in as states," he said; "you'll have to swallow every last one of them."[6] The question was thus squarely raised and faced as one of the admission of territories not intended for statehood.

The debate over this was long and voluminous. Much of it was concerned with legalities. But these were not the real issue. The real issue was one of expediency and wisdom. The proponents of expansion advanced a variety of arguments. Some said that it was our _manifest destiny_ to acquire these territories. Others said that for one reason or another we had a paramount interest in them. Still others maintained that we, as an enlightened and a Christian nation, had a duty to regenerate their ignorant and misguided inhabitants. Another argument was that they were necessary to the defense of our continental territory. Finally, it was alleged by the commercially minded that we had to take them, Hawaii and the Philippines in particular, to assure ourselves of a fitting part in what was regarded as the great future trade with the Orient.

The opponents of expansionism argued partly in legal terms, challenging the constitutionality of such arrangements. But their most powerful arguments were those which asked by what right we Americans, who had brought our country into

6. R. Cortissoz, _Life of Whitelaw Reid_ (New York, 1921), II, 266. From a letter of January 22, 1900, to Senator William E. Chandler.

existence on the thesis that governments derive their just powers from the consent of the governed, could assume the rights of empire over other peoples and accept them into our system, regardless of their own feelings, as subjects rather than as citizens. To annex foreign territory and govern it without the consent of its population, said Senator Hoar of Massachusetts in the course of the debate over the ratification of the peace treaty with Spain, would be utterly contrary to the sacred principles of the Declaration of Independence and unconstitutional because it promoted no purpose of the Constitution. The Founding Fathers, said the Senator, had never thought that their descendants "would be beguiled from these sacred and awful verities that they might strut about in the cast-off clothing of pinchbeck emperors and pewter kings; that their descendants would be excited by the smell of gun powder and the sound of the guns of a single victory as a small boy by a firecracker on some Fourth of July morning."[7]

The strongest argument of the imperialists was actually none of those that I mentioned but the argument of what has sometimes been called contingent necessity—the argument that, unless we took these territories, somebody else would and that this would be still worse. In the case of Puerto Rico and Hawaii, this argument seems to me to have been unsubstantial. There was no real likelihood of anybody else intervening. Puerto Rico could quite safely have been left with Spain, or given independence like Cuba, so far as our security was concerned. In the case of the Philippines the question was a more serious one. Once we had completed our defeat of the Spanish forces on the island and the conquest of Manila, once we had shattered Spanish rule, there was no question of giving the islands back to Spain. It was also fairly clear that the inhabitants were hardly fit for self-rule, even if there had been a chance of their being let alone by other powers, which there

7. Cited by Julius W. Pratt, *Expansionists of 1898* (Baltimore, 1936), p. 347.

was not. The alternative to our taking them would probably have been a tussle between England and Germany over their possession but with a reasonable likelihood that some sort of a *modus vivendi* and division of the territory would eventually have resulted. Sooner or later, the Japanese would also have become competitors for their possession. Whether this would have been unfortunate from the standpoint of later developments in the Southwest Pacific, I cannot say. The historian's power fails before such speculative questions. But if we today cannot see a likelihood that this would have been particularly unfavorable to America's interests, I doubt that the people of that time could have seen it very clearly themselves. And if they did not, one asks one's self, why did they need to destroy Spanish reign in the islands at all?

The Russian writer, Anton Chekhov, who was also a doctor, once observed that when a large variety of remedies were recommended for the same disease, it was a pretty sure sign that none of them was any good and that the disease was incurable. Similarly, when one notes the variety of arguments put up by the expansionists for the territorial acquisitions of 1898, one has the impression that none of them was the real one—that at the bottom of it all lay something deeper, something less easy to express, probably the fact that the American people of that day, or at least many of their more influential spokesmen, simply liked the smell of empire and felt an urge to range themselves among the colonial powers of the time, to see our flag flying on distant tropical isles, to feel the thrill of foreign adventure and authority, to bask in the sunshine of recognition as one of the great imperial powers of the world. But by the same right of retrospect one is impressed with the force and sincerity of the warnings of the anti-expansionists and the logic, as yet never really refuted, of their contention that a country which traces its political philosophy to the concept of the social compact has no business taking responsibility for people who have no place in that concept and who are supposed to appear on the scene in the role of subjects and not of citizens. Kings can have subjects; it is a question whether a republic can.

One remembers, in particular, the words of one of the anti-imperialists, Frederick Gookin: "The serious question for the people of this country to consider is what effect the imperial policy will have upon ourselves if we permit it to be established."[8] It is primarily in the light of this question that one thinks about our subsequent experience with these colonial possessions.

About Puerto Rico, I shall not speak. Recent events have surely been eloquent enough to cause us all to ask ourselves whether we have really thought through all the implications of a relationship so immensely important, so pregnant with possibilities for both good and evil, as the colonial tie between our country and the people of Puerto Rico. In the case of Hawaii, we see the outcome of the decision as a relatively successful one, but only, I fear, because American blood and American ways were able to dominate the scene entirely: because the native way of life was engulfed and reduced, as was the case with our American Indians, to the helpless ignominy of tourist entertainment. In the case of the Philippines, we recall that only a few years after their annexation the first and most eager protagonist of their acquisition, Theodore Roosevelt, was already disillusioned, was already repenting his initiative and wishing we could be rid of them. Finally, let us remember, in the thirties we decided to set them free, and we recently did so, but not really primarily for their sake—not primarily because we were sorry for them or thought them prepared for freedom and felt that we had an obligation to concede it to them—but rather because we found them a minor inconvenience to ourselves; because the economic intimacy that

8. Frederick W. Gookin, *A Literary Catechysm* (Chicago, 1899), p. 17, as cited by A. K. Weinberg, *Manifest Destiny* (Baltimore, 1935), p. 306.

their existence under our flag implied proved uncomfortable to powerful private interests in this country; because, in other words, we were not ourselves prepared to endure for long even those rudimentary sacrifices implied in the term "the white man's burden." Remember Gookin's words which I just cited: "The . . . question . . . is what effect the imperial policy will have upon ourselves."

When one thinks of these things, one is moved to wonder whether our most signal political failures as a nation have not lain in our attempts to establish a political bond of obligation between the main body of our people and other peoples or groups to whom, whether because we wished it so or because there was no other practical solution, we were not in a position to concede the full status of citizenship. There is a deep significance in the answer to this question. If it is true that our society is really capable of knowing only the quantity which we call "citizen," that it debauches its own innermost nature when it tries to deal with the quantity called "subject," then the potential scope of our system is limited; then it can extend only to people of our own kind—people who have grown up in the same peculiar spirit of independence and self-reliance, people who can accept, and enjoy, and content themselves with our institutions. In this case, the ruling of distant peoples is not our dish. In this case, there are many things we Americans should beware of, and among them is the acceptance of any sort of a paternalistic responsibility to anyone, be it even in the form of military occupation, if we can possibly avoid it, or for any period longer than is absolutely necessary.

These, then, are some of the things that strike us when we think about the remote and picturesque conflict with Spain at the end of the last century. Let us recapitulate them.

We see that, in the reasons governing our resort to war and the determination of the character of our military operations, there was not much of solemn and careful deliberation, not much prudent and orderly measuring of the national interest.

When it came to the employment of our armed forces, popular moods, political pressures, and inner-governmental intrigue were decisive. McKinley did not want war. But, when the bitter realities were upon him, there is no indication that either he or his Secretary of State felt in duty bound to oppose the resort to war if this was advantageous to them from the standpoint of domestic politics. Having resorted to war for subjective and emotional reasons, we conducted it in part on the basis of plans which, as far as we know, had never been seriously examined and approved by any competent official body; which were known to, and understood by, only a tiny handful of individuals in the government service; and which obviously reflected motives ulterior to the announced purposes of the war as defined by Congress. When the success of the naval and military operations that flowed from these plans inflamed public imagination and led to important questions of the acquisition of foreign territory, the Executive branch of the government took little part in the debate. It made no serious effort to control the effects of popular reaction to the exploits of a popular commander far afield. It was only the obligation of the Senate to ratify treaties which caught the tremendous issues involved and brought them to the attention of the public in a senatorial debate as measured and enlightened as any we have ever had.

To my mind it seems unlikely, in the light of retrospect, that the conclusions which triumphed in that debate were the right ones. But we should not let that constitute a reproach to our forefathers, for we are poor judges of their trials and predicaments. Let us content ourselves with recording that in the course of their deliberations they stumbled upon issues and problems basic to the health of our American civilization; that these issues and problems are ones which are still before us and still require answer; and that, whereas the men of 1898 could afford to be mistaken in their answers to them, our generation no longer has this luxury.

II

MR. HIPPISLEY AND THE OPEN DOOR

✱

IN THE first of these lectures I spoke about the Spanish-American War as a sort of preface to the diplomacy of the first half of the twentieth century. I wish now to talk about another episode in American diplomatic history, from those same years at the turn of the century, an episode which had this same preface-like quality: the dispatch of John Hay's Open Door notes.

I think you will all remember the general nature of this occurrence, as it has been usually understood in this country. It was something like this: At a time when the European powers were setting about to partition China and to appropriate parts of it to their exclusive use, the American Secretary of State, surmising their purposes, anticipated them and in part frustrated their design by sending them notes which called them to observe in China the principle of the Open Door—the principle of equal rights for all, that is—and of the territorial and administrative integrity of China. The interpretation put upon this incident by public opinion at the time and carried down into the textbooks of our own day is well summed up by Mark Sullivan in his study entitled *Our Times:*

The "open-door" policy in China was an American idea. It was set up in contrast to the "spheres-of-influence" policy practised by other nations. . . .

The "open-door" is one of the most creditable episodes in American diplomacy, an example of benevolent impulse accompanied by energy and shrewd skill in negotiation. Not one of the statesmen and nations that agreed to Hay's policy wanted to. It was like asking every man who believes in truth to stand up—the liars are obliged to be the first to rise. Hay saw through them perfectly; his insight into human nature was one of his strongest qualities.[1]

Now, bearing in mind this interpretation, let us take a closer look at what really happened.

At the end of 1897 and the beginning of 1898 there was a real and justifiable fear that China would be partitioned. It was in those months that the Russians made evident their determination to have a special position in Manchuria, including a naval base at Port Arthur and a commercial port at the present Dairen, both to be connected by railway with the new Trans-Siberian; that the Germans consolidated their control over the port of Kiaochow and their influence in the Shantung Peninsula; and that the French, coming up from the south, from the present Indochina, successfully negotiated with the Chinese government for the lease of a port, for railroad concessions, for the appointment of a French citizen as head of the Chinese postal services, and for other favors.

These happenings naturally caused particular concern in London. Up to that time the British had been the overwhelming masters of the Chinese trade. They had 80 per cent of it; all the rest of the countries together, including ourselves, had only 20 per cent. Being in a favorable competitive position, British traders had always advocated the Open Door in China —that is, equality for everyone in customs treatment, harbor dues, etc., for the importation of consumption merchandise. Now they were not certain how this would all work out with these spheres of influence that other powers were acquiring. Would this operate to exclude British trade or would it not?

This was not a simple question. Up to that time the main difficulties in the China trade had been with the local Chinese authorities in the interior, not with the actions of foreign powers. British merchants had long demanded of their own

1. Mark Sullivan, *Our Times: The Turn of the Century* (New York, 1926), p. 509.

government that it ignore diplomatic proprieties, ignore the Chinese government in Peking, go right into the interior of China, up the great rivers, with its gunboats, and force the stubborn mandarins to remove the obstructions and exactions which they placed in the path of the movement of merchandise. If this was what the other powers were going to do in their spheres of influence, perhaps it was a good thing. Perhaps the British could even profit from it. But suppose those powers just opened up the interior to trade and kept it to themselves. Then things would be worse than ever.

The British government, itself, as distinct from the British merchants, had other worries arising out of these events— worries more serious than the complaints and anxieties of British commercial circles. These worries were strategic and political. British statesmen did not like the idea of a Russian naval base on the Gulf of Pechili. Where would all this end? Would it not lead to complete Russian domination of China? The British Foreign Office spoke its fears quite frankly in a secret communication to the czar's government:

A great military Power which is coterminus for over 4,000 miles with the land frontier of China, including the portion lying nearest to its capital, is never likely to be without its due share of influence on the councils of that country. Her Majesty's Government regard it as most unfortunate that it has been thought necessary in addition to obtain control of a port which, if the rest of the Gulf of Pechili remains in hands so helpless as those of the Sovereign Power, will command the maritime approaches to its capital, and give to Russia the same strategic advantage by sea which she already possesses in so ample a measure by land.[2]

The Russians paid no attention to this communication and went right ahead with the realization of their plans. After considerable worry and debate the British government responded to this situation in the spring of 1898 in two ways:

2. *British Documents on the Origins of the War, 1898–1914* (London, 1927), I, 28.

openly, by stressing the importance of the maintenance of the Open Door in China; covertly, by looking about for some sort of special agreement with some other power or powers for opposing Russia's strategic penetration of Chinese territory. But in the back of their minds they had still a third line of action, a line which they were somewhat reluctant to take at that time but which was being strongly pressed upon them by many of the British merchants in China and which they knew they would have to take if neither of the other methods worked— that was the development of a sphere of influence of their own in the Yangtze Valley, where their own trade was greatest and where they, too, would be able to exert a more direct influence on the government at Peking. By developing such a sphere of influence, they could at least make sure that they would not be excluded from the most important part of China, and there might be other advantages besides.

In the spring of 1898 they still hoped—as I say—that it would not come to this, but they could not be too sure. Things were changing in China. The Open Door doctrine, the basis of British policy for many years, was beginning to show its limitations generally. In the old days it had been only a question of bringing in consumption goods for general distribution and sale. For such trade the Open Door principle had been clearly applicable and had suited British interests. But now foreign countries were interested in acquiring concessions from the Chinese government for railway construction and mining enterprises. Here, the Open Door principle did not really seem applicable. Such concessions were too important, strategically and politically, for anyone to expect that the Chinese government should be guided only by commercial considerations in granting them. The Chinese government was practically forced to decide in which areas of China it wanted one power to build railways and in which areas another. And there was a good deal to be said for keeping the powers somewhat apart geographically in their concession activities, not all milling around together. If the British wanted to get in on the concession business, which they did, it was almost essential that they stake out a sphere where their concessions would be concentrated and the concessionaires of other powers excluded.

So there was a deeper logic and necessity behind the growth of these so-called spheres of influence than merely the wickedness of the powers themselves. The Open Door doctrine—a doctrine so old that it was referred to in the British Parliament in 1898 as "that famous phrase that has been quoted and requoted almost *ad nauseam*"[3]—was simply not fully relevant to the new situation. However, the British government thought it still useful to talk about the Open Door and press publicly for its acknowledgment, because trade in consumption goods was still importantly involved, as well as concessions; they did not want to see British merchants excluded anywhere; and, if the principle of commercial "openness" were to be generally respected, this might act as a certain restraint on the expansion of the strategic and political influence of the other powers.

It was against this background that the British government, in March, 1898 (about a month before the outbreak of the Spanish-American War), made its one and only formal approach to the United States government about the Open Door doctrine. It sent a secret communication to President McKinley, pointing out the danger that other powers might annex portions of Chinese territory or lease them under conditions which would assure themselves preferential treatment, and asking "whether they could count on the cooperation of the United States in opposing any such action by Foreign Powers and whether the United States would be prepared to join with Great Britain in opposing such measures should the contin-

3. *Parliamentary Debates* (4th ser., 1898), LXIV, 827 (August 10: remarks of Balfour).

gency arise."[4] Please note that they did not come out against spheres of influence. <u>They came out only against annexations or leases of territory under conditions that would exclude the trade of other nations.</u>

There is no evidence that the British Foreign Office attached much importance to this approach or had much hope for its success. The British diplomats were more interested in other overtures they were making about the same time—to Japan and Germany. The approach to us had apparently been pressed upon them by the Colonial Minister, Joseph Chamberlain. Chamberlain, who had an American wife, had high hopes for Anglo-American political co-operation. He was powerful in domestic politics and took a prominent part in the conduct of foreign policy. I suspect that he had been needling the Foreign Office about enlisting American co-operation in China and that the Foreign Office sent the note to our government largely to satisfy him, perhaps even to demonstrate that there was nothing in the idea; but that is only a conjecture.

In any case, nothing came of it at the time. Washington was preoccupied with the Cuban problem. The Department of State did not even have a Far Eastern Division in those days. The Secretary of State, old John Sherman, was inactive, somewhat senile, and about to give over his job. <u>Washington said, in effect, "Nothing doing"</u>; and the matter was not again raised in any formal way by the British government.

As I say, one <u>cannot be sure that the British Foreign Office was particularly disappointed with this answer. But there was one man who was. He was John Hay, our ambassador to Lon</u>don. He was absent from London when the approach was made, traveling in Egypt with his friend Henry Adams. When he returned and heard what had happened, he sat down and wrote to the <u>Secretary of State asking for a reconsideration of</u>

4. Cited in Alfred Vagts, *Deutschland und die Vereinigten Staaten in der Weltpolitik* (New York, 1935), II, 1029. Vagts gives the State Department archives as the source.

our decision, only to be told that the time was still inopportune.

Hay was presumably interested in the matter exclusively from the standpoint of our relations with England. He knew little if anything about China; he had never been there. But he thought that we were unwise not to be sympathetic to the British in a situation where we might help them and perhaps thereby build up a sort of diplomatic credit on which we could draw later.

In late summer of that year Hay was appointed Secretary of State. Unquestionably, when he came home to assume his duties, he had this matter on his mind. Some of the British had continued to talk to him about it from time to time during the summer, particularly Chamberlain. But, actually, British policy itself was beginning to move quietly away from the Open Door doctrine and continued to do so through the winter of 1898–99. The British statesmen still did lip service to the Open Door principle; but, recognizing that spheres of influence were not to be done away with so easily or to be spurned from the standpoint of their own interests, they proceeded quietly to take certain precautionary measures of their own. To balance the Russian position at Port Arthur, they leased a strategic port on the other side of the Gulf of Pechili. They went into the railway concession business in a big way, particularly in the Yangtze Valley. And they did one more thing which is particularly worth noting in connection with this subject we are discussing today. That was the leasing of Kowloon.

As you will remember, they already had the island of Hongkong as a Crown colony. From there they did business with the mainland of China. I fear that a certain amount of that business may have been irregular in the sense that it evaded payment of the Chinese customs duties; in other words, it was smuggling. Now the Chinese Imperial Maritime Customs Service was at that time an international service administered with great vigor, honesty, and efficiency by an Englishman, Sir Robert Hart. Hart's integrity was such that he did not hesitate to step on the British merchants in China as hard as on anyone else who came into conflict with the customs regulations. Under his uncompromising and rigorous administration the Customs Service, which had acquired some revenue cutters, encircled Hongkong and kept movement between the island and the mainland under strict observation. It was apparently partly as a counter to this that the British, in June, 1898, acquired a lease on a portion of the Chinese mainland across the strait from Hongkong—the piece of territory known as Kowloon. With Kowloon in their possession it would be possible for goods to pass from Hongkong to the mainland without customs supervision. And it is significant that one of their first acts after acquiring the territory was to close the customhouse of the Chinese Imperial Maritime Customs. This was naturally a source of concern to Sir Robert Hart and the Customs Service. With the Germans and the Russians, they had thus far had no trouble. The Germans had even invited them to set up a customhouse in their port of Kiaochow, where there had not been one before. But Hart was very apprehensive about what the Russians might do in the future. If the British were going to set this sort of a precedent, by expelling the Customs Service from Kowloon, and if the precedent were followed by others, then the establishment of the spheres of influence might conceivably lead to the closing of customhouses everywhere in the so-called spheres of influence, to the complete breakup of the Customs Service itself, and to the financial ruin of the Chinese government.

When John Hay took up his duties as Secretary of State in the late months of 1898, he had no adviser on Far Eastern affairs. He therefore brought back to Washington a friend of his, W. W. Rockhill. Rockhill was then minister to Greece. He had served in China before, but it was seven years since he had been there, and he was somewhat out of touch with conditions. Although we have no direct evidence of this fact, we may at least suppose that what Hay wanted him to do was to find some way of responding to the British request that we help them in their China problem.

Rockhill got back in the spring of 1899 but apparently was not immediately able to recommend any action along this line. There is some evidence that the President was still averse to taking any such action. In his message to Congress, in December, 1898, he had spoken as though the problem were one which had largely solved itself. We are also justified in suspecting that Rockhill himself did not know just how to tackle the problem—what action to take. The British were not renewing their request about the Open Door; they showed very little interest in it, as a matter of fact. The British ambassador, following the good old custom of that day, went away to Newport for the summer and was not available for consultation. Actually, as we have seen, the British government was slipping rapidly away from the Open Door policy in their actions in China and probably had no desire at that time to be reminded of it.

Then events began to happen. In the middle of June there arrived in the Washington area an old friend of Rockhill's from Peking: an Englishman by the name of Hippisley, who was second in command of the Chinese Customs Service, under Sir Robert Hart. Hippisley was on leave of absence from his post in China and was passing through the United States on his way to England. His wife was a Baltimore girl and a friend of Mrs. Rockhill. Presumably still smarting under the effect of the British action at Kowloon, and imbued with the necessity of preserving the authority of the Imperial Maritime Customs Service over the importation of goods into China, he urged that the American government "do what it can to maintain the Open Door for ordinary commerce in China."[5] Spheres of interest, he said, were there to stay and had to be treated as existing facts. So long as they were taken to apply only to railroad and mining concessions, it was all right. But if people began to extend this concept to customs treatment, dangers would arise. With this in view he urged that the United States approach the other European powers and get from each of them an assurance that they would not interfere with treaty ports in their spheres of influence (that is, with ports where the Imperial Maritime Customs Service had its establishments) and that the Chinese treaty tariff should apply without discrimination to all merchandise entering their respective spheres of influence.

Rockhill was taken with these ideas. But at first he thought they were unfeasible from the domestic political standpoint. So did Hay, who was then on vacation in New Hampshire but who remained in correspondence with Rockhill about the matter. "I am fully awake to the great importance of what you say," Hay wrote to Rockhill on August 7, "and am more than ready to act. But the senseless prejudices in certain sections of the 'Senate and people' compel us to move with great caution."

Shortly after this, however, things suddenly changed. For one reason or another the domestic political inhibitions to taking action seem to have been overcome. On August 24, Hay gave Rockhill authorization to go ahead with Hippisley's suggestion. Basing his position largely on a memorandum drafted by Hippisley, Rockhill drew up a paper which was presented to the President and approved by him. On the basis of this paper, in turn, a series of notes were drawn up, addressed to the various powers which had interests in China.

5. The correspondence among Hay, Rockhill, and Hippisley on this subject is cited extensively in A. Whitney Griswold, *The Far Eastern Policy of the United States* (New York, 1938), chap. ii; all references to this correspondence are taken from that source.

Hay came down from New Hampshire long enough to sign the notes; they were duly dispatched; Hay returned to his vacation in New Hampshire; and the summer doldrums once more settled over Washington.

The notes began with a discussion of the background. This discussion embodied some of Hippisley's thoughts but also included some of Rockhill's own ideas. It contained a refusal by the United States government to recognize the spheres of influence at all, whereas Hippisley had said they were there to stay and that there was no use challenging them. But the kernel of the notes lay in a concrete three-point formula, quite technical in wording, which was taken almost verbatim from Hippisley's memorandum. There is no evidence that this formula was given any serious critical study in the United States government or that any effort was made to assess the practical significance it would have when measured against events in China. It seems to me likely, in view of its origin and wording, that it was a carefully prepared summary of the desires of the Chinese Imperial Maritime Customs Service at that particular moment. It also seems likely that it was really aimed largely at the British.[6] By getting our government to sponsor it, Hippisley had obviously found a convenient roundabout way of putting pressure on the British government to behave in a manner less threatening to the interests of the Customs Service in China. But there is no indication that either Rockhill or John Hay was aware of this aspect of the matter or had any idea of the extent to which Hippisley's formula might be in conflict with British policy at that particular moment. That they suspected the British of sideslipping a bit from the straight-and-narrow path of the Open Door seems probable. I would doubt, however, that they understood how far this deviation

6. The first of the three articles had primary relevance to the British sphere of influence, in which the great bulk of the establishments of the Imperial Maritime Customs Service was situated.

had gone and how little agreeable to the British would be the formula contained in the notes.

The reception given to the notes by the various governments was tepid, to say the least. The British failed to register enthusiasm, bickered for a long time about the application of the formula to Kowloon, and finally gave a conditional assent—that is, they would subscribe to our principles to the extent that everybody else might subscribe to them. Since everybody else made the same condition, the replies were no stronger than their weakest link. The weakest link was obviously Russia. The language of the Russian reply was cryptic and evasive. Our ambassador at St. Petersburg warned Hay that the Russian government "did not wish to answer your propositions at all. It did so finally with great reluctance."[7] Despite this warning—so reminiscent of many warnings which were later to be given by the American Embassy in Moscow against placing too much faith in verbal assurances wormed out of the Soviet government—Hay did not hesitate to announce, on March 20, 1900, that he had received satisfactory assurances from all the powers and that he regarded them as "final and definitive."[8] He thereby gave the impression, which the American public was not slow to accept, that the European powers, who had been on the verge of getting away with something improper in China, had been checked and frustrated by the timely intervention of the United States government and that a resounding diplomatic triumph had been achieved.

In doing this, incidentally, he created a precedent which was destined to bedevil American diplomatic practice for at least a half-century thereafter and may—as far as I can see—continue to bedevil it for another half-century still. We shall see in the next of these lectures something of the nature and significance of this precedent.

7. Cited in Tyler Dennett, *John Hay* (New York, 1934), p. 294.
8. *Foreign Relations of the United States, 1899* (Washington, 1901), p. 142.

This was not all that there was to the story of the Open Door notes. There was an epilogue. Hay's announcement that he had received satisfactory assurances from the foreign powers about the Open Door principle happened to coincide almost exactly with the beginning of the Boxer Rebellion. This was, as you will recall, a violent and fanatical anti-foreign movement, in part connived at by the Chinese government, which led to much destruction of foreign property, to the killing of a number of foreigners, to the flight of thousands more from the interior, and to a full-fledged military attack on the foreign legations in Peking, who were surrounded and besieged and forced to defend themselves with arms over a period of several weeks, until relieving expeditions reached the city.

It was a presidential election year in the United States. The siege of the legations in Peking began on June 20 and ended on August 14. The Republican National Convention met in Philadelphia on June 19 and the Democratic Convention in Kansas City on July 4. The air was already ringing with controversies about "imperialism," which grew out of the decisions surrounding the Spanish-American War. The administration felt no desire to be drawn any more deeply than necessary into military ventures in China or to be harassed that summer by any further explosive issues of foreign policy. On July 3, one day before the opening of the Democratic National Convention, Hay issued to the powers another circular, this time defining—in what were apparently intended to be soothing and noncontroversial terms—American policy toward China in the light of the existing disorder and anarchy in that country. In the first Open Door notes he had mentioned the desirability of maintaining the integrity of China but had not stressed this point. Now, in the circular of July 3, 1900, it was specifically stated that "the policy of the Government of the United States is to seek . . . to preserve Chinese territorial and administrative entity."[9] This reference to the territorial and admin-

9. *Foreign Relations of the United States, 1900* (Washington, 1903), p. 299.

istrative "entity" of China has been taken by historians as adding a new note to the thoughts put forward in the original Open Door communications and as committing this government to the protection of China against foreign encroachments on her territory. That was indeed to be the interpretation put upon it and followed by the United States government for most of the next fifty years. The Open Door notes are thus generally considered to have been those addressed to the powers in the summer of 1899 plus the circular issued during the Boxer Rebellion in the following summer.

Actually, none of these communications had any perceptible practical effect. The later circular, in fact, was scarcely noticed at all outside our own country. There was little reason to expect that things would be otherwise. The Boxer Rebellion, accompanied as it was by foreign military intervention, was bound to lead to a net increase, rather than decrease, in the authority exerted by foreign governments in China. The Russians used it to strengthen their hold on Manchuria. And the indemnities levied against the Chinese government forced the latter to increase its borrowings from one or the other of the powers, and hence its dependence on them.

The authors of the American Open Door policy soon became themselves quite disillusioned with it. It seemed to be almost swallowed up in the march of events. To Hippisley, the Boxer Rebellion meant the inevitable breakup of China, which in turn meant the end of the Open Door. Rockhill, who was sent out to Peking as a special United States commissioner to help reorganize Chinese affairs after the rebellion, is said to have written, only two years after the first Open Door notes were sent: "I trust it may be a long time before the United States gets into another muddle of this description."[10]

As for Hay himself, in December, 1900, only five months after his proclamation of devotion to the principle of upholding Chinese territorial and administrative "entity," he se-

10. Griswold, *op. cit.*, p. 83.

cretly instructed our minister in Peking to try to obtain for the
United States a naval coaling station at Samsah Bay in the
Chinese province of Fukien.[11] But when, a few weeks later, the
Japanese, alarmed by the increasing pace of Russian encroach-
ment in Manchuria, inquired politely whether the United
States would be inclined to join them in using force to assure
the observance of the principles it had enunciated, Hay replied
that the United States was "not at present prepared to attempt
singly, or in concert with other Powers, to enforce these views
in the east by any demonstration which could present a character of hostility to any other Power."[12]

There is every reason to believe that the Japanese took the
most careful and attentive note of the significance of this statement. They were interested then, as always, in real military
allies, not half-hearted ones. One year later they signed the
Anglo-Japanese alliance on which their security was to be
based for many years to come. Three years later they took up
arms and threw the Russians out of the south of Manchuria.
In doing these things, they neither expected our aid nor feared
our opposition. Had not Hay said that our views about China
were not ones which we would enforce by any demonstration
which could present a character of hostility to any other
power?

These, then, were the circumstances surrounding the issu-
ance of John Hay's Open Door notes. When you analyze them,
what did they amount to? It seems to me that they amounted
to something like this.

In the summer of 1899 the American Secretary of State approached a number of other powers and asked them to subscribe to a certain formula designed to govern the policies of
countries that had acquired spheres of influence in China.

It was not a formula which Hay had drafted. There is no

11. *Foreign Relations of the United States, 1915* (Washington, 1924), pp. 113–14.

12. State Department memorandum of February 1, 1901, cited by Alfred L. P. Dennis
in *Adventures in American Diplomacy* (New York, 1928), p. 242.

evidence that he understood fully its practical significance. One of his assistants had bought it sight unseen, so to speak, from an Englishman who had happened to be in the vicinity of Washington that summer. It was probably thought to be responsive to a request the British had made of us. Actually, it did not represent English policy of the moment; it was even somewhat in conflict with that policy. It may have represented the aspirations of the Chinese Imperial Maritime Customs Service in the face of certain developments which threatened its future. It was not a new policy but an old one. It was not an American policy but one long established in British relations with China. It was not a policy that in general had a future; it was an antiquated one, already partially overtaken by developments. It was not a policy that we Americans cared enough about to support in any determined way or for the results of which, if implemented, we were prepared to accept any particular responsibility. Finally, as events were shortly to show, it was not even a policy to which we ourselves would be inclined to adhere in our own possessions, for within a few years after our acquisition of the Philippines and Puerto Rico —and despite our brave promises to the contrary—we set up discriminatory regimes, conflicting with the Open Door principle, in both of these newly acquired territories.

There is no evidence that Hay was aware of these realities, in so far as they were the realities of the moment, or was capable of foreseeing them, in so far as they pertained to the future. There is perhaps no reason to suppose that he should have. The formula had a high-minded and idealistic ring; it would sound well at home; it was obviously in the interests of American trade; the British had been known to advocate it— still did, so far as he knew—and it was hard to see what harm could come from trying it on the other powers. This he did. He got the grudging, embarrassed, and evasive replies which might have been expected. He was warned of the lack of substance in these replies, but he saw no reason why he should not turn to the American public and make the best of it by representing these answers as a diplomatic success.

For all this, I do not blame him and do not mean to censure him. He was a man of his time—a man of dignity and sensitivity—a great American gentleman. He labored in a framework of government which was unsuited, really, to the conduct of the foreign affairs of a great power. He was making the best of an unsatisfactory situation.

But what I do want to stress, and this is the central point of this discussion, is that the American public found no difficulty in accepting this action as a major diplomatic achievement. Its imagination was fired, its admiration won. Hay was established in its affections as a great statesman. The popularity of the administration's foreign policy was materially improved just at the time of the coming presidential elections.

Not only was this effect achieved at the moment, but a myth was established which was destined to flourish in American thinking for at least a half-century. Neither the obvious lack of practical results, nor the disillusionment of Hay and the other persons involved, nor our unwillingness to bolster the policy in any forceful way, nor our subsequent departure from it ourselves—none of these things succeeded in shaking in any way the established opinion of the American public that here, in this episode of the Open Door notes, a tremendous blow had been struck for the triumph of American principles in international society—an American blow for an American idea.

III

AMERICA AND THE ORIENT

☼

IN THE second of these lectures I took for examination a single episode in American diplomacy, the Open Door notes of John Hay. Let us now look back at the entire subsequent series of events in our Far Eastern policy.

The history of American foreign policy in the Far East during these last fifty years is a long and complicated story. Only a very erudite man could say that he had read and digested even the major part of the material relevant to the subject or could hold in his mind's eye the entire panorama of events and all the aspects of the complicated framework of circumstance in which they took place.

I can make no such claim. I have no personal familiarity with that part of the world. I have read no more than a busy person, not an expert on Far Eastern affairs, can contrive to read in the face of other interests and obligations. And if it should seem in an academic setting unscholarly, or perhaps not even useful, to examine this subject against such a background, I can only say that this is precisely what the policymakers in Washington, for the most part, have to do. The heart of their problem lies—and will always lie—in the shaping and conduct of policy for areas about which they cannot be expert and learned. What we are about to do today is therefore to share, so to speak, in their experience.

The importance of the Open Door incident lay largely in the fact that it introduced a pattern destined to become characteristic of American diplomacy for forty years into the future. During this entire period the burden of our song would continue to be the Open Door and the preservation of the territorial and administrative integrity of China. Time after time we would call upon other powers to make public confession of their adherence to these principles. Time after time we would receive from them reluctant, evasive, or qualified replies, putting us on notice that no one would deny the principles but that it all depended on how they were interpreted. Time after time we would present these replies to our own people, despite their qualified nature, as diplomatic achievements: as acknowledgments of the justice of our view, expressions of contrition, evidences of willingness to reform. In no instance would we admit that this sort of intervention in the affairs of the other powers in China carried with it any specific responsibility for us or placed us under obligation to anybody or anything but our own consciences. In no instance would we be prepared to use force to compel compliance with these principles or to protect individual powers if they complied with them and others failed to do so. And, finally, as in the case of the Hay notes, our constant return to these ideas, though irritating and sometimes puzzling to the other powers, would not serve really to prevent the conflicts of interests in China from living themselves out pretty much in accordance with their own strategic, political, and economic necessities. It would not prevent, in other words, much of that happening which was bound to happen. But toward the end of this period it would come dangerously close to the most vital interests of some of the powers, notably Japan, and would contribute to the establishment of emotional attitudes among their peoples which would be of great importance to the security and fortunes of our country.

If this, then, was to be the basic pattern of our policy in the Far East for four decades and perhaps even longer, let us have a closer look at some of its components.

First of all, the principles. We noted in the second of these lectures that the term "Open Door" was already an old and hackneyed one at the turn of the century. It had been used mainly with reference to the treaty ports. Its principal significance was simply that in those ports where foreigners had the privilege of residing, trading, and maintaining warehouses and office facilities under a special regime of protection trade should be opened to the vessels and nationals of all foreign countries alike. What was involved here was the introduction into China of general consumption merchandise—textiles, in particular—for sale to the interior. And we saw that this principle was not fully relevant to the new problems involved in the opening-up of China for such things as the construction of railways and the development of minerals—a process which began roughly at the turn of the century. The truth of the matter is that the circumstances surrounding foreign business activity in China from 1900 on were so complex, so varied, and in many instances so contradictory that no two-word formula or symbol could possibly have had any plain and comprehensive meaning adequate as a criterion for international agreement on a large number of practical questions. Attempts were occasionally made to define the principle in greater detail, as in the original Open Door notes and in the Nine-Power Treaty negotiated at the Washington Conference. But none of these definitions could really embrace anything so diffuse, so many-sided, and so little susceptible to expression in Western semantics as the economic interests and activities of the foreign powers in China.

The same was true of "the territorial and administrative integrity of China." This seemed to Western observers, on the face of it, a plain and specific principle. But this view assumed that China was at all times a nation like other nations, with all the qualifications essential to a neat embodiment in the national state system as it had grown up in the West. Actually, the facts were not this simple. China was a state, of course, in the sense of its being a political entity of immense importance to the world—an entity which had to be taken into account and studied and dealt with by the Western powers. But there were many ways in which its attributes failed to coincide with the clear pattern of the national state in an international context, as evolved in Europe in the eighteenth and nineteenth centuries. China's government came only late and imperfectly to the acceptance of the principle of equality among sovereigns. The nature of its authority in various parts of the realm did not always fully correspond to what is assumed by Western concepts of the state in the law of nations. Accordingly, there was frequently confusion over the question of responsibility for the enforcement on the Chinese side of engagements entered into with the Western powers. Where local authorities wanted to obstruct fulfilment of these engagements, the Chinese government was not always able to compel compliance. Difficulties of language, outlook, and custom added to this confusion. Chinese standards and institutions of justice, while not necessarily inferior to those of the West, were strange, incomprehensible, and unacceptable to many foreigners in China. This meant a choice in many instances between special regimes and privileges for foreigners or the total abstention of those foreigners from residence and activity in China. And while, in many cases, the presence and activity of foreigners in China had undoubtedly been pressed upon the Chinese authorities by measures that were unwise if not unjust, there were many other instances in which the Chinese either encouraged and connived at this or adopted toward it an ambiguous attitude that made idle any search for ultimate moral justifications or reproaches. The fact of the matter was that by the end of the century there had grown up in China an extremely complicated and delicate set of relationships between the Chinese and the governments and nationals of other powers—a set of relationships that defied adequate definition in Western terms. And if one had been asked at that time whether these arrangements were compatible with "the administrative and territorial integrity of China," one could only have shrugged one's shoulders and asked in reply: What's in a name? It depends on what you call integrity.

This was particularly true, we might note, of Manchuria, about which much of the controversy concerning the application of these principles was to revolve, and where our efforts to assure their observance would someday become particularly intensive and important. Manchuria was not, historically speaking, a part of old China. The Chinese relation to it had been a somewhat indirect one, running through the Manchus. At the turn of the century much of Manchuria represented both for China and for Russia a semideveloped frontier area. Both countries had important interests in it. The Chinese had nominal sovereignty, and the area was rapidly filling up with Chinese pioneers and colonists. But it occupied a geographic position of unquestionable strategic importance to Russia. Once the Russians undertook, as they did in the 1890's, to build a railroad across Siberia to the Pacific Ocean, the Russian interest in northern Manchuria was established. It was idle to deny it or to expect it to disappear behind a polite deference to Western concepts of state sovereignty and international amenities. We must bear in mind that the administrative and technical vigor of Chinese government at the turn of the century was not adequate either to the construction of railways in northern Manchuria or to the provision of a suitable framework of administrative protection for such railways as might be constructed. And once China had consented to the building of the Chinese Eastern Railway by the Russian government, a significant degree of Russian administrative and strategic influence in the area tapped by that railway was inevitable.

The attainment of this position in northern Manchuria naturally gave the Russians new facilities for projecting their influence into the southern part of Manchuria as well as Korea and northern China. The events following the Sino-Japanese War of 1895 showed that the Russians would not be averse to exploiting these possibilities. They also showed that the Chinese government, as it existed at that time, was not able to mount effective resistance to these efforts and to prevent Russian domination of these additional areas. The only practical alternative to Russian power on the Gulf of Pechili was at that time Japanese power, not Chinese. The British recognized this. This was one of the basic factors in the circumstances that lay behind the conclusion of the Anglo-Japanese Alliance in 1902. It lay behind the Russo-Japanese War that followed in 1904–5. The result of that war, as you will recall, was that the Japanese replaced the Russians as the dominant power in South Manchuria and Korea but did not interfere with nominal Chinese sovereignty in the area, any more than the Russians had interfered with it in the north. This arrangement, which emanated from the outcome of the Russo-Japanese War and endured until the Russian Revolution temporarily shattered Russia's power in the area, proved to have considerable stability, and one is moved to conclude that it must have borne a fairly accurate relationship to the power realities and requirements of the area. At any rate, there were no discernible alternatives to it that promised any greater stability, and even our own reiteration of our devotion to the principle of Chinese territorial and administrative integrity was punctuated by occasional admissions from American statesmen that the arrangement was not altogether a bad thing. Theodore Roosevelt recognized as desirable, as early as 1905, that a balance should be preserved between Russia and Japan in that area "so that each may have a moderating action on the other,"[1] and he said at a later date:

It is . . . peculiarly our interest not to take any steps as regards

1. *Selections from the Correspondence of Theodore Roosevelt and Henry Cabot Lodge*, II, 153.

Manchuria which will give the Japanese cause to feel, without reason, that we are hostile to them, or a menace—in however slight a degree—to their interests. . . . I do not believe in our taking any position anywhere unless we can make good; and as regards Manchuria, if the Japanese choose to follow a course of conduct to which we are adverse, we cannot stop it unless we are prepared to go to war, and a successful war about Manchuria would require a fleet as good as that of England, plus an army as good as that of Germany. The Open Door policy in China was an excellent thing, and I hope it will be a good thing in the future, so far as it can be maintained by general diplomatic agreement; but, as has been proved by the whole history of Manchuria, alike under Russia and under Japan, the "Open Door" policy, as a matter of fact, completely disappears as soon as a powerful nation determines to disregard it, and is willing to run the risk of war rather than forego its intention.[2]

In accordance with these views our government found little difficulty in reconciling itself to the establishment of Japanese predominance in Korea. And the Taft-Katsura and Root-Takahira agreements of 1905 and 1908, respectively, whatever they may have meant to us, surely meant to the Japanese an implicit recognition of the position they had acquired in Manchuria.

These considerations suffice, I think, to show that neither of the phrases "Open Door" or "administrative and territorial integrity of China" had any clear applicability to actual situations in China in the sense that they could have been said to indicate feasible and practical alternatives to all the special positions and interests of the powers in that country. It was not that the principles were wrong; it was not that they had in them no elements of soundness or that truth and justice were all on the other side. Unquestionably, in these foreign positions in China there was much that was of reprehensible origin, much that had been extorted from the helplessness of the Chinese, much that it might have been wiser for foreigners not

2. Cited by A. Whitney Griswold, *The Far Eastern Policy of the United States*, pp. 131-32.

to have sought and acquired. Unquestionably, there would continue to be new foreign undertakings in China which the United States would be warranted in viewing with concern and disapproval and in declining, for its own part, to have anything to do with or any responsibility for. But this was not the point; the trouble with the Open Door doctrine and the integrity of China as political principles was simply that these terms were not clear and precise ones which could usefully be made the basis of a foreign policy. To a large extent they were clichés, dangerously inexact and confusing in the associations they provoked in people's minds. It was precisely this aspect of their character which made it difficult for other governments, when summoned by us to stand up and be counted in their feelings about them, to do anything else but reply: "Why, yes, if you put it that way, we agree, of course." These phrases contained too many positive overtones to be safely rejected outright by anyone. It was easier to agree than to try to explain.

The fact of the matter is that these phrases had meaning only in relation to specific situations in China. You would have had to explain in each case what you meant by them. It cannot be said that they had any adequate and practical generic meaning. An attempt to apply them literally and schematically could only have meant a complete abstention of foreigners in general from residence and activity in China—and a policy of having nothing to do with China at all, as a sort of punishment or reward, however you might look at it, for China's obstinacy in refusing to fit into the Western state system. We can believe, as I am inclined to do, that this might have been not a bad thing; that its ultimate results, at any rate, might have been preferable to what we have before us today. But it was hardly a practical suggestion at any time after the turn of the century from the standpoint of any of the Western powers.

So much, then, for our principles. Now a word or two about their implementation.

We have noted that, when we summoned other powers to declare their adherence to these principles, there were good reasons why they would agree to do this, but there were also reasons why their replies would almost invariably be guarded and qualified ones hemmed in with significant reservations. This being the case, we may ask ourselves how useful it was to solicit such replies and to hold them before the American public as definite diplomatic accomplishments. The instances in which this was done are so numerous that I shall not attempt to recite them. They have not been confined to Far Eastern affairs. The tendency to achieve our foreign policy objectives by inducing other governments to sign up to professions of high moral and legal principle appears to have a great and enduring vitality in our diplomatic practice. It is linked, certainly, with the strong American belief in the power of public opinion to overrule governments. It is also linked, no doubt, with the pronounced American tendency to transplant legal concepts from the domestic to the international field: to believe that international society could—and should—operate on the basis of general contractual obligation, and hence to lay stress on verbal undertaking rather than on the concrete manifestations of political interest. But in the Far Eastern field this diplomatic device seems to have achieved the status of a basic diplomatic method, and I think we have grounds to question its soundness and suitability. It was bound to work a certain abuse on public understanding of international realities in our own country; for time and again people were given the impression of a community of outlook among nations which did not really exist. But more serious, I think, was the bewilderment, suspicion, and concern which it must have caused in the foreign mind. Foreign statesmen were keenly aware of the inadequacy of these general propositions as definitions of any workable agreement or understanding on specific international issues. Assuming, as they must have assumed, that our government was also aware of this, it must have been difficult for them not to suspect our statesmen of holding back and of having ulterior motives in pressing these abstractions upon them as criteria of agreement.

And this leads me to the second, and more important, reservation that I would raise concerning our policy in the Far East. This applies particularly to our relations with Japan in the years between the two wars, when the Japanese became the main target of our diplomatic pressures and reproaches in that area. This reservation is with regard to our general reluctance to discuss specific arrangements as well as general principles and, above all, our reluctance to suggest—or take responsibility for—practical alternatives to the courses of action which we opposed. Remember that the bulk of our diplomatic activity was activity designed to deflect other powers, notably the Japanese, from the pursuit of specific courses of action we did not like. The fact that a compliance with our views might have had serious consequences of a practical nature for them and for China, that it might have raised new problems and inconveniences or even have produced an actual disbalance of the power factors in that area, and that this might in turn have involved a responsibility on our part and a right of others to call upon us to do specific things in the exercise of that responsibility, seems rarely to have occurred to us. So far as I can judge from such evidence as I have seen, it was assumed by American statesmen that whatever was uttered or urged in the name of moral or legal principle bore with it no specific responsibility on the part of him who urged it, even though the principle might be of questionable applicability to the situation at hand and the practical effects of adherence to it drastic and far-reaching. We were at liberty to exhort, to plead, to hamper, to embarrass. If others failed to heed us, we would cause them to appear in ungraceful postures before the eyes of world opinion. If, on the other hand, they gave heed to our urgings, they would do so at their own risk; we would not feel bound to help them with the resulting problems—they were on their own.

It was in this spirit that we hacked away, year after year, decade after decade, at the positions of the other powers on the mainland of Asia, and above all the Japanese, in the unshakeable belief that, if our principles were commendable, their consequences could not be other than happy and acceptable. But rarely could we be lured into a discussion of the real quantities involved: of such problems as Japan's expanding population, or the weaknesses of government in China, or the ways in which the ambitions of other powers could be practicably countered. Remember that this struck a particularly sensitive nerve in the case of countries whose interests on the Asiatic mainland were far more important to them than our interests there were to us. No one likes to receive suggestions for alterations of his behavior from someone who obviously has far less to lose than he has from the consequences of such an alteration. There was always a feeling, both among the Japanese and among the British, that we were inclined to be spendthrift with their diplomatic assets in China for the very reason that our own stake in China meant so much less to us than theirs did to them.

Nor would we, over the space of many years, often consent to take into account the significance of what we were asking from the standpoint of Japanese internal affairs. If the price of our frustration of Japan's policies on the mainland was the final entrenchment of the power of the military extremists at Tokyo, that apparently made little difference over the long run. There were of course important exceptions to this in the sense that American statesmen tried hard, at times, to adjust American policy in such a way that it would affect favorably the situation in Japan. But these were efforts that ran counter to the tide and were not characteristic of the sum total of American policy. It made little difference if our desiderata touched Japanese feelings in peculiarly sensitive spots. It made little difference that the Japanese soul already bore the wounds of having been deprived of the fruits of victory by outside force after the war with China in 1894. We would not let that worry us when we allowed ourselves to appear again at the conclusion of the war with Russia in 1905 as the frustrators of Japanese victory (which we really were not). We would not let it interfere with our rushing in again, in the wake of World War I—this time as the real leaders of a determined movement to deprive Japan of what she conceived to be the fruits, in terms of betterment of her position on the mainland, of her participation in the war against Germany.

And none of this would be improved by the fact that throughout this long and unhappy story we would repeatedly irritate and offend the sensitive Japanese by our immigration policies and the treatment of people of Japanese lineage, and of oriental lineage in general, in specific localities in this country. The federal government was prepared to plead with local authorities in California and elsewhere for a recognition of the element of national interest in these unhappy problems of residence, of landownership, of neighborhood treatment; but it was not prepared to force any issues; and the country as a whole remained unwilling to recognize that the actions and attitudes of state and local authorities might constitute an important element in the creation of foreign policy. Least of all were we willing to agree that the troubles arising over these matters gave us cause to be more moderate in our other demands on Japan.

Now, these are bitter reflections, and I would not have them misunderstood. The march of events in the Far East in the decades prior to World War II was a vast and turgid process, involving immensely powerful currents of human affairs over which we Americans had little control or influence. It is easy to overrate the importance of the part we played, or the part we could have played, in this process. It is also easy to exaggerate the latitude our statesmen enjoyed—to forget the political and psychological framework in which they operated, the inadequacy of the instruments at their disposal, the domestic impediments to other and more promising lines of approach. What I have said is not intended as reproach to them, for none of us is fully able to put himself in their place, and it is not important to us to pass judgment on them as individuals.

I cannot tell you that all would have been different had we been guided by other principles of conduct. I cannot say that Pearl Harbor might have been avoided had we been over a long period of time more circumspect in our attitudes toward the Japanese, more considerate of the requirements of their position, more ready to discuss their problems with them on their own terms. Least of all can I point to any single act of American policy and say: Here was the thing that did it—this was the thing that tipped the scales of the future. In the fabric of human events, one thing leads to another. Every mistake is in a sense the product of all the mistakes that have gone before it, from which fact it derives a sort of a cosmic forgiveness; and at the same time every mistake is in a sense the determinant of all the mistakes of the future, from which it derives a sort of a cosmic unforgiveableness. Our action in the field of foreign policy is cumulative; it merges with a swelling stream of other human happenings; and we cannot trace its effects with any exactness once it has entered the fluid substance of history. I suspect that in the developments leading to World War II in the Pacific there must have been a dividing line between the phase when something hopeful could still have been accomplished by our own efforts and the phase when circumstances were beyond repair—the point at which sheer tragedy overtook human frailty as the determinant of our misfortunes. But I cannot promise you that there was such a point, and I certainly cannot tell you where it lay.

I can only say that if there was a possibility that the course of events might have been altered by an American policy based consistently, over a long period of time, on a recognition of power realities in the Orient as a factor worthy of our serious respect, and directed toward the stability and quietness as well as the legal and moral tidiness of the situation there—if there was, as I say, a possibility that the course of events might have been altered by such a policy, then it must be admitted that we did very little to exploit this possibility, to give it a chance to become reality, to derive from it such benefit as could have been derived for our own interests and for those of world peace.

And I would add that the need for giving this possibility a chance is not just hindsight. There were qualified observers who questioned long before World War II the adequacy of a policy oriented increasingly toward the undermining of the positions of the foreign governments in China and the frustration of Japan's interests on the mainland. One of our best informed professional diplomats, Mr. John V. A. MacMurray, retired since several years, wrote in 1935 an extremely thoughtful and prophetic memorandum, in which, pointing to the likelihood of a war with Japan if we continued in the course we were following, he observed that even the most drastic achievement of our objectives in such a war would only play into the hands of Russia and raise a host of new problems.

The defeat of Japan would not mean her elimination from the problem of the Far East . . . a virile people . . . are not made tractable by defeat and national humiliation; they tend, rather, to reassert themselves with a passionate impulse of self-esteem, by methods which may well give them . . . a "nuisance value"—scarcely if at all less potent than the force which they exerted in their prime of imperial power. But even the elimination of Japan, if it were possible, would be no blessing to the Far East or to the world. It would merely create a new set of stresses, and substitute for Japan the U.S.S.R. as the successor to Imperial Russia—as a contestant (and at least an equally unscrupulous and dangerous one) for the mastery of the East. Nobody except perhaps Russia would gain from our victory in such a war. . . . If we were to "save" China from Japan . . . [it] is no reproach to the Chinese to acknowledge that we should have established no claim upon their gratitude; nations and races collectively do not seem in general to be susceptible to that sentiment. . . . They would thank us for nothing, and give us no credit for unselfish intentions, but set themselves to formulating resistance to us in the exercise of responsibilities we would have assumed.

These words need no other commentary than the situation we have before us today in Korea. It is an ironic fact that today our past objectives in Asia are ostensibly in large measure achieved. The Western powers have lost the last of their special positions in China. The Japanese are finally out of China proper and out of Manchuria and Korea as well. The effects of their expulsion from those areas have been precisely what wise and realistic people warned us all along they would be. Today we have fallen heir to the problems and responsibilities the Japanese had faced and borne in the Korean-Manchurian area for nearly half a century, and there is a certain perverse justice in the pain we are suffering from a burden which, when it was borne by others, we held in such low esteem. What is saddest of all is that the relationship between past and present seems to be visible to so few people. For if we are not to learn from our own mistakes, where shall we learn at all?

Looking backward over a half-century of American diplomacy in the Far East, we see curious phenomena which undoubtedly have their origin in our own emotional complexes. We see a distinct difference between our policy toward this area and our policy toward Europe. We see in our approach to the Orient a lack of those inhibitions which long affected us in our approach to the affairs of the European continent. We find ourselves more willing to accept involvement in oriental affairs, less inclined to dismiss them as of no moment to us.

On the other hand, we find no greater readiness, so far, to admit the validity and legitimacy of power realities and aspirations, to accept them without feeling the obligation of moral judgment, to take them as existing and inalterable human forces, neither good nor bad, and to seek their point of maximum equilibrium rather than their reform or their repression.

Unquestionably, our relation to the peoples of the Far East has been colored by a certain sentimentality toward the Chinese—a sentimentality as disrespectful to them and as unhelpful to the long-term interests of our relations as the feelings of blind petulance into which it now has a tendency to turn. In general, we expect too much from our Asian friends in the way of intimacy and mutual liking. There is something patronizing in this attitude of ours. We have never really thought through the full connotations of our domestic practices and habits of thought for our relations with the peoples of Asia. No people can be the judge of another's domestic institutions and requirements, and we have no need to be apologetic to anyone, unless it be ourselves, for the things we do and the arrangements we enforce within our own country. But it would seem that a nation which admits that its own capacity for assimilation is limited once you get beyond the peoples of Caucasian origin should observe a special reserve in its dealings with other peoples and in its hopes for intimacy of association with them.

I cannot resist the thought that if we were able to lay upon ourselves this sort of restraint and if, in addition, we were able to refrain from constant attempts at moral appraisal—if, in other words, instead of making ourselves slaves of the concepts of international law and morality, we would confine these concepts to the unobtrusive, almost feminine, function of the gentle civilizer of national self-interest in which they find their true value—if we were able to do these things in our dealings with the peoples of the East, then, I think, posterity might look back upon our efforts with fewer and less troubled questions.

IV

WORLD WAR I

✣

LET me recall once more the nature of the enterprise we are
embarked upon in this series of lectures. This is not an
attempt to recount a sequence of events, to report the development of new historical fact, or to give a rounded picture of
America's diplomacy over fifty years. It is an attempt to look
back from a present full of uncertainty and controversy and
unhappiness, to see whether a study of the past will not help
us to understand some of our present predicaments.

We have now come, in the course of this undertaking, to
what seems to me the most baffling, most tragic, and—for the
historian—most challenging of all the phases of human events
encountered in the record of this period. By this I mean the
terrible, prolonged, and wasteful struggle that we know as
World War I—and all that went with it.

I would like first to say a word about the total result of these
two world wars in Europe. These wars were fought at the
price of some tens of millions of lives, of untold physical destruction, of the destruction of the balance of forces on the
Continent—at the price of rendering western Europe dangerously, perhaps fatefully, vulnerable to Soviet power. Both
wars were fought, really, with a view to changing Germany:
to correcting her behavior, to making the Germans something
different from what they were. Yet, today, if one were offered
the chance of having back again the Germany of 1913—a Germany run by conservative but relatively moderate people, no

Nazis and no Communists, a vigorous Germany, united and unoccupied, full of energy and confidence, able to play a part again in the balancing-off of Russian power in Europe—well, there would be objections to it from many quarters, and it wouldn't make everybody happy; but in many ways it wouldn't sound so bad, in comparison with our problems of today. Now, think what this means. When you tally up the total score of the two wars, in terms of their ostensible objective, you find that if there has been any gain at all, it is pretty hard to discern.

Does this not mean that something is terribly wrong here? Can it really be that all this bloodshed and sacrifice was just the price of sheer survival for the Western democracies in the twentieth century? If we were to accept that conclusion, things would look pretty black; for we would have to ask ourselves: Where does all this end? If this was the price of survival in the first half of the twentieth century, what is survival going to cost us in the second half? But plainly this immense output of effort and sacrifice should have brought us something more than just survival. And then, we can only assume, some great miscalculations must have been made somewhere? But where? Were they ours? Were they our Allies?

Eclipsed for many of us by the fresher and more vivid recollections of World War II, this first World War has become in many respects the forgotten factor. Yet all the lines of inquiry, it seems to me, lead back to it. World War II seemed really so extensively predetermined; it developed and rolled its course with the relentless logic of the last act of a classical tragedy. And the main elements of that tragic situation—the sickness and impatience of Germany, the weakness of eastern Europe, the phenomenon of bolshevism in Russia, and the weariness and debility in France and England—all these things took their origin so clearly in the period of 1914–20 that it seems to be here, if anywhere, that the real answers should be sought.

I do not mean to say that there were not still important things that could have been done in the twenties and the thirties, or perhaps even in the forties, to avert the worst dangers and to press the stream of events into more hopeful channels. Thirty years is a long time in the course of human events. The life of an international community can always be inclined to some extent, like a tree, by persistent pressure in a single direction over a long space of time.

But I would submit that a significant narrowing of the choices of the generations from 1920 to 1950 began with the outbreak of violence in 1914; that with the subsequent emergence of a military deadlock and the disappearance of hopes for a compromise peace this process was greatly advanced; and that by the time the fire of war had finally burned itself out, and the Treaty of Versailles had been signed, the area in which Western statesmen, and above all American statesmen, could act to restore genuine health and peace to Western civilization, and to give that civilization strength to withstand the growing challenge from the East, had been grievously and tragically narrowed.

So we come back to the fact that much of the cause for the decline in our security in the West lay with the course and outcome of the first World War. And for this reason our own part in it deserves the most careful scrutiny.

What was the problem for our statesmen? Let us review it again in our minds.

You all remember how war broke out in 1914. The origins of this war were complex in the extreme. I will not try to describe them in detail here. Some were of a long-term nature: the still-unsolved problems of the breakup of the old Turkish Empire, the restlessness of subject peoples in the Danubian basin, the loss of what the French call the *élan vital* in Austria-Hungary, the relative growth of German power, the rivalry between Germany and England. Others were of a short-term nature:

the stupidities and timidities of statesmen, the pressures of public opinion, the vagaries of coincidence. If you tried to compute the various degrees of guilt, you got a rather fuzzy pattern: the Austrians and the Russians no doubt in first place, the Germans with less but certainly with a goodly share, and no one with none at all. Above all, you could not say that anyone had deliberately started the war or schemed it. It was a tragic, helpless sort of war from the beginning. Poor old Europe had got herself into a box. The structure of her international life had a weak spot. The shot at Sarajevo struck into that weak spot—and suddenly no one knew how *not* to go to war.

About the course of the war, once it had started, you also need little instruction from me. The course of it was as tragic and as nonsensical as its origin. The deadlock was not long in establishing itself on the western front, and it is hard today to visualize the full hideousness and wastefulness of what ensued: those four long years of miserable carnage; that appalling phenomenon of great armies of men facing each other in the muddy trenches day after day, month after month, year after year, destroying each other hopelessly, systematically, with artillery barrages, with the as yet unanswered weapon of the machine gun, with trench mortars and barbed wire and even poison gas, until victory or defeat came to seem less a product of military leadership and skill and spirit than a matter of some grisly mathematics of cannon fodder and slaughter. "The fire," wrote Winston Churchill in 1929, "roared on till it burned itself out."

Events passed very largely outside the scope of conscious choice. Governments and individuals conformed to the rhythm of the tragedy, and swayed and staggered forward in helpless violence, slaughtering and squandering on ever-increasing scales, till injuries were wrought to the structure of human society which a century will not efface, and which may conceivably prove fatal to the present civilization. . . .[1]

"Injuries were wrought to the structure of human society which a century will not efface." Churchill knew what he was saying when he wrote those words. The injuries were deeper than most people ever dreamed at the time. You could fill in the old trenches. You could plow up the fields of Flanders, where the poppies grew. You could rebuild the French towns. Life could begin to look normal again after a few years. But there were trenches no one could fill, fields where no poppy would ever grow again, structures no one could ever rebuild. They were in the souls of the men who took part in that war— the survivors. And what can one say of the six million who never came back?

I wonder if any of you remember the final passages of Remarque's *All Quiet on the Western Front*—the greatest novel of the first World War. I am going to read them to you because I think they have a place in any discussion of that war, and they bring out something I can convey to you in no other way. Imagine to yourselves a young German GI in a military hospital behind the German lines, in the autumn of 1918, shortly before the end of the war.

It is autumn. There are not many of the old hands left. I am the last of seven fellows from our class.

Everyone talks of peace and armistice. All wait. If it again proves an illusion, then they will break up; hope is high, it cannot be taken away again without an upheaval. If there is not peace, then there will be revolution.

I have fourteen days rest, because I have swallowed a bit of gas; in a little garden I sit the whole day long in the sun. The armistice is coming soon, I believe it now, too.

Here my thoughts stop and will not go any further. All that meets me, all that floods over me are but feelings—greed of life, love of

1. Winston Churchill, *The World Crisis, 1915* (New York, 1929), pp. 1–2.

home, yearnings of the blood, intoxication of deliverance. But no aims.

Had we returned home in 1916, out of the suffering and strength of our experiences we might have unleashed a storm. Now if we go back we will be weary, broken, burnt out, rootless, and without hope. We will not be able to find our way any more.

And men will not understand us—for the generation that grew up before us, though it has passed these years with us here, already had a home and a calling; now it will return to its old occupations, and the war will be forgotten—and the generation that has grown up after us will be strange to us and push us aside. We will be superfluous even to ourselves, we will grow older, a few will adapt themselves, some others will merely submit, and most will be bewildered; —the years will pass by and in the end we shall fall into ruin.

.   .   .   .

Here the trees show gay and golden, the berries of the mountain ash stand red among the leaves, country roads run white out to the skyline, and the canteens hum like beehives with rumors of peace.

I stand up.

I am very quiet. Let the months and years come, they bring me nothing, they can bring me nothing. I am so alone and so without hope that I can confront them without fear. The life that has borne me through these years is still in my hands and eyes. Whether I have subdued it, I know not. But so long as it is there it will seek its own way out, heedless of the will that is within me.[2]

Now that was World War I. Those of you here who are veterans may say: "Why, that wasn't just World War I. . . . That was any war." Right you are. And if there was anything special about the first World War, it was only that the thing went on in the same way and in the same places for an awfully long time; there was not much movement, not much adventure, not much hope that anything could happen that would change the whole fortunes of war at any early date. The losses were terrific on both sides. You could practically calculate

2. Erich Maria Remarque, *All Quiet on the Western Front*, trans. A. W. Wheen (Boston: Little, Brown & Co., 1929; London: Putnam & Co., Ltd., 1929), p. 290.

when your time would come. And it was all so unutterably futile.

But the words of this German soldier are important because there was written in them not just the feelings of many fighting men toward the end of the war but also something of the pattern of the future. In these words you read practically everything that was to come: the maladjustment of the veteran's generation; the gap in the age groups; the older men (the Chamberlains, the Hindenburgs, the Pétains) who did not understand the postwar world and who were nevertheless required to wield power in it and to hold that power too long; the younger men who grew up full of frustration, insecurity, and bewilderment and who, as Remarque correctly observed, would some day be strange to the veterans and push them aside. Here was the forecast of the strength of totalitarianism, and the fatigue of democracy, in the period between the wars.

Now it would be pleasant, and would ease our task, if we could say that, as a war so sickening ran its course, peoples and governments on both sides sobered and became thoughtful, became aware of the increasing emptiness of victory, aware that no political objectives could be worth this price, amenable to any reasonable suggestion for a compromise peace that would put an end to the slaughter. Unfortunately, we cannot say this. There are certain sad appreciations we have to come to about human nature on the basis of the experiences of these recent wars. One of them is that suffering does not always make men better. Another is that people are not always more reasonable than governments; that public opinion, or what passes for public opinion, is not invariably a moderating force in the jungle of politics. It may be true, and I suspect it is, that the mass of people everywhere are normally peace-loving and would accept many restraints and sacrifices in preference to the monstrous calamities of war. But I also suspect that what purports to be public opinion in most countries that consider themselves to have popular government is often not really the consensus of the feelings of the mass of the people at all but rather the expression of the interests of special highly vocal minorities—politicians, commentators, and publicity-seekers of all sorts: people who live by their ability to draw attention to themselves and die, like fish out of water, if they are compelled to remain silent. These people take refuge in the pat and chauvinistic slogans because they are incapable of understanding any others, because these slogans are safer from the standpoint of short-term gain, because the truth is sometimes a poor competitor in the market place of ideas—complicated, unsatisfying, full of dilemmas, always vulnerable to misinterpretation and abuse. The counsels of impatience and hatred can always be supported by the crudest and cheapest symbols; for the counsels of moderation, the reasons are often intricate, rather than emotional, and difficult to explain. And so the chauvinists of all times and places go their appointed way: plucking the easy fruits, reaping the little triumphs of the day at the expense of someone else tomorrow, deluging in noise and filth anyone who gets in their way, dancing their reckless dance on the prospects for human progress, drawing the shadow of a great doubt over the validity of democratic institutions. And until peoples learn to spot the fanning of mass emotions and the sowing of bitterness, suspicion, and intolerance as crimes in themselves—as perhaps the greatest disservice that can be done to the cause of popular government—this sort of thing will continue to occur.

In 1916 people in Europe had not yet learned this, any more than many people in the United States have learned it today; and, by consequence, the progress of World War I did not bring reasonableness, or humility, or the spirit of compromise to the warring peoples. As hostilities ran their course, hatreds congealed, one's own propaganda came to be believed, moderate people were shouted down and brought into disrepute, and war aims hardened and became more extreme all around.

The Allies came to be interested only in a total victory over Germany: a victory of national humiliation, of annexations, of crushing reparations. They resented suggestions for an end of hostilities on any other basis.

The Germans wanted to retain military facilities in Belgium. They wanted to hold Belgium for the future in the status of a subordinate state. They wanted a slight increase in their own territory, for economic reasons, at the expense of France. They wanted an indemnity for evacuating France and Belgium. These aims were of course utterly unacceptable to the Allies.

Now, plainly, all this posed no easy problem for American statesmanship, and I would not want it thought that anything I am about to say indicates any lack of sympathy for Woodrow Wilson or of appreciation for the depth and bitterness of his problems. But none of this absolves us from the duty of looking coldly and critically at the nature of our national reaction to such a challenge.

In the first place, with respect to the origins of the war: let us note that there was for long no understanding in this country that either the origins or the issues of the war were of any concern to us. Speaking in 1916, President Wilson said that with the objects and causes of the war "we are not concerned. The obscure foundations from which its stupendous flood has burst forth we are not interested to search for or explore."[3] "America," he said on a later occasion, "did not at first see the full meaning of the war. It looked like a natural raking out of the pent-up jealousies and rivalries of the complicated politics of Europe."[4] Here, we may note, there was no recognition

3. Address to the First Annual Assemblage of the League To Enforce Peace, May 27, 1916.

4. Speech on the "S.S. George Washington," July 4, 1919.

that what might be at issue in the European war was anything that concerned us. There was the same denial we saw in the case of the Far East—of the legitimacy of the real interests and aspirations of other peoples, the same dismissal of these things as unsubstantial and unworthy of our attention, as "jealousies and rivalries" too silly, too "complicated," to deserve our respect.

Proceeding on this basis, it was logical that the only American interest in the war we were inclined to recognize for a long time was the defense of our neutral rights according to the established laws of maritime warfare, as they had been known in the past. We did not understand that new modalities of warfare and new weapons—above all, the total blockade and the submarine—had rendered obsolete some of the more important of these rules. Not only had their observance become physically impracticable, but each side had come to feel that its chances of victory and survival depended on the violation of one or another of them. Either side would have preferred to accept war with us rather than refrain from violating certain ones of them. This meant that a strict insistence by us on their observance could eventually lead us, theoretically, into war with both belligerents—a paradoxical ending for a policy designed to keep us out of war.

Looking backward today on these endless disputes between our government and the belligerents over neutral rights, it seems hard to understand how we could have attached so much importance to them. They irritated both belligerents and burdened our relations with them, and I find it hard to believe that they involved our national honor. It might be our privilege to defend the rights of our citizens to travel on belligerent vessels, but it was hardly a duty, unless we chose to define it as a duty to ourselves.

As time went on, there grew up, of course, alongside this outlook, something quite different: a realization of the danger of defeat that confronted the Entente powers and an awareness of the damage that would be done to our world position by the elimination of England as a strong force in the world. In addition to this, the superiority of British propaganda, and other factors, began to work to the benefit of the Allied cause. The result was a gradual growth of pro-Allied sentiment, and particularly in the minds of the responsible American leaders. This sentiment was enough to cause Wilson and House to water down our neutrality policy to the benefit of the British and to make cautious efforts to stop the war, in 1915 and 1916, as the best means of averting the danger of a British defeat. But this pro-Ally feeling was never sufficient to constitute, for the national consciousness as a whole, adequate justification for entering the war; and you will remember that our entry, when it came, was over an issue of neutrality.

Once in the war, we had no difficulty in discovering—and lost no time in doing so—that the issues involved in it were of the greatest significance to us.

It is surely a curious characteristic of democracy: this amazing ability to shift gears overnight in one's ideological attitudes, depending on whether one considers one's self at war or at peace. Day before yesterday, let us say, the issues at stake between ourselves and another power were not worth the life of a single American boy. Today, nothing else counts at all; our cause is holy; the cost is no consideration; violence must know no limitations short of unconditional surrender.

Now I know the answer to this one. A democracy is peaceloving. It does not like to go to war. It is slow to rise to provocation. When it has once been provoked to the point where it must grasp the sword, it does not easily forgive its adversary for having produced this situation. The fact of the provocation then becomes itself the issue. Democracy fights in anger—it fights for the very reason that it was forced to go to war. It fights to punish the power that was rash enough and hostile enough to provoke it—to teach that power a lesson it will not forget, to prevent the thing from happening again. Such a war must be carried to the bitter end.

This is true enough, and, if nations could afford to operate in the moral climate of individual ethics, it would be understandable and acceptable. But I sometimes wonder whether in this respect a democracy is not uncomfortably similar to one of those prehistoric monsters with a body as long as this room and a brain the size of a pin: he lies there in his comfortable primeval mud and pays little attention to his environment; he is slow to wrath—in fact, you practically have to whack his tail off to make him aware that his interests are being disturbed; but, once he grasps this, he lays about him with such blind determination that he not only destroys his adversary but largely wrecks his native habitat. You wonder whether it would not have been wiser for him to have taken a little more interest in what was going on at an earlier date and to have seen whether he could not have prevented some of these situations from arising instead of proceeding from an undiscriminating indifference to a holy wrath equally undiscriminating.

In any case, once we were at war, it did not appear to us that our greatest danger might still lie precisely in too long a continuation of the war, in the destruction of Europe's equilibrium, and in the sapping of the vital energies of the European peoples. It did not appear to us then that the greatest interest we had in the war was still that it should be brought to an end as soon as possible on a basis involving a minimum maladjustment and as much stability as possible for the future. Prior to our entry into the war, many people had thought that way. As late as January, 1917, Wilson was still arguing against total victory. A "peace forced upon the loser, a victor's terms imposed upon the vanquished," he said, "would be accepted in humiliation, under duress, at an intolerable sacrifice, and would leave a sting, a resentment, a bitter memory upon

which terms of peace would rest . . . as upon quicksand."[5]
But, once we were in the war, these ideas were swept away by
the powerful currents of war psychology. We were then as
strong as anybody else in our determination that the war
should be fought to the finish of a total victory.

Considerations of the power balance argued against total
victory. Perhaps it was for this very reason that people in this
country rejected them so emphatically and sought more sweeping and grandiose objectives, for the accomplishment of which
total victory could plausibly be represented as absolutely essential.[6] In any case, a line of thought grew up, under Wilson's
leadership, which provided both rationale and objective for
our part in fighting the war to a bitter end. Germany was militaristic and antidemocratic. The Allies were fighting to make
the world safe for democracy. Prussian militarism had to be
destroyed to make way for the sort of peace we wanted. This
peace would not be based on the old balance of power. Who, as
Wilson said, could guarantee equilibrium under such a system?
It would be based this time on a "community of power," on
"an organized common peace," on a League of Nations which
would mobilize the conscience and power of mankind against
aggression. Autocratic government would be done away with.
Peoples would themselves choose the sovereignty under which
they wished to reside. Poland would achieve her independence, as would likewise the restless peoples of the Austro-
Hungarian Empire. There would be open diplomacy this time;
peoples, not governments, would run things. Armaments
would be reduced by mutual agreement. The peace would be
just and secure.

In the name of such principles you could fight a war to the

5. Address to the Senate, January 22, 1917.

6. This was not true of Wilson—at least in the beginning of 1917. His mind was able
to entertain simultaneously thoughts of peace without victory and expansive concepts
of a future world order which explicitly rejected the balance of power.

end. A future so brilliant would surely wash away the follies and brutalities of the war, redress its injuries, heal the wounds it had left. This theory gave us justification both for continuing the war to its bitter and terrible end—to the end described by that young German soldier in the military hospital—and at the same time for refusing to preoccupy ourselves with the practical problems and maladjustments to which the course of hostilities was leading. Under the protecting shadow of this theory, the guns continued their terrible work for a final year and a half after our entry. Under the shadow of this theory Wilson went to Versailles unprepared to face the sordid but all-important details of the day of reckoning. Under this theory he suffered his tragic and historic failure. Under this theory things advanced with a deadly logic and precision to a peace which was indeed "forced upon the loser, a victor's terms imposed upon the vanquished, accepted in humiliation, under duress"—a peace that did indeed leave a sting, a resentment, a bitter memory, and upon which its own terms came later to rest "as upon quicksand."

And the tragedy of this outcome was not substantially mitigated by the fact that we were not signatories to the Treaty of Versailles and kept ourselves aloof from its punitive provisions. The damage had been done. The equilibrium of Europe had been shattered. Austria-Hungary was gone. There was nothing effective to take its place. Germany, smarting from the sting of defeat and plunged into profound social unrest by the breakup of her traditional institutions, was left nevertheless as the only great united state in Central Europe. Russia was no longer there, as a possible reliable ally, to help France contain German power. From the Russian plain there leered a single hostile eye, skeptical of Europe's values, rejoicing at all Europe's misfortunes, ready to collaborate solely for the final destruction of her spirit and her pride. Between Russia and Germany were only the pathetic new states of eastern and

Central Europe, lacking in domestic stability and the traditions of statesmanship—their peoples bewildered, uncertain, vacillating between brashness and timidity in the exercise of the unaccustomed responsibilities of independence. And to the other side of Germany were France and England, reeling, themselves, from the vicissitudes of the war, wounded far more deeply than they themselves realized, the plume of their manhood gone, their world positions shaken.

Truly, this was a peace which had the tragedies of the future written into it as by the devil's own hand. It was a peace, as the French historian Bainville said, which was too mild for the hardships it contained. And this was the sort of peace you got when you allowed war hysteria and impractical idealism to lie down together in your mind, like the lion and the lamb; when you indulged yourself in the colossal conceit of thinking that you could suddenly make international life over into what you believed to be your own image; when you dismissed the past with contempt, rejected the relevance of the past to the future, and refused to occupy yourself with the real problems that a study of the past would suggest.

But suppose you hadn't taken this line. Would things have been different? Was there another line you could take?

It does seem to me there was.

You might have begun, I should think, with a recognition of the importance to us of what was brewing in Europe in those years before the outbreak of war. You will remember that Wilson dismissed all this as something we were not even interested to examine.

Yet, was it all so silly, so unworthy of attention? I said in the beginning that some of the causes of the war were deep ones. The absence of a major war on the Continent during the century before 1914 had rested on a balance of power which presupposed the existence of France, Germany, Austria-Hungary, and Russia as dominant elements—and all of this flanked by an England instinctively conscious of her stake in the preservation of the balance among them and prepared to hover vigilantly about the fringes of the Continent, tending its equilibrium as one might tend a garden, yet always with due regard for the preservation of her own maritime supremacy and the protection of her overseas empire. In this complicated structure lay concealed not only the peace of Europe but also the security of the United States. Whatever affected it was bound to affect us. And all through the latter part of the nineteenth century things were happening which *were* bound to affect it: primarily the gradual shift of power from Austria-Hungary to Germany. This was particularly important because Austria-Hungary had not had much chance of becoming a naval and commercial rival to England, whereas Germany definitely did have such a chance and was foolish enough to exploit it aggressively, with a chip on her shoulder, in a way that gave the British a deep sense of concern and insecurity.

It is not only in retrospect that these things are visible.

In the winter of 1913 there appeared, anonymously, and in an English magazine (because no American magazine would take it), an article written by an American diplomatist of the time, Mr. Lewis Einstein.[7] In this article, Mr. Einstein drew attention to the storm clouds gathering over Europe, to the depth of the Anglo-German antagonism, to the danger that war might arise from some relatively insignificant incident, and to the effect that such a war might have on the equilibrium and stability of Europe. He then went on to trace out the significance of such a European war for the security of the United States. He never doubted that we would have to intervene to save England, if the alternative were clearly her destruction. But he warned against the assumption that we would not be affected by any drastic alteration either way in the balance of forces in Europe:

7. *National Review*, LX (January, 1913), 736–50.

Unperceived by many Americans, the European balance of power is a political necessity which can alone sanction on the Western Hemisphere the continuance of an economic development unhandicapped by the burden of extensive armaments.

. . . The disappearance or diminution of any one state in Europe would be a calamity, varying with its degree. . . .

It is no affair of the United States even though England were defeated, so long as the general balance is preserved. But if ever decisive results are about to be registered of a nature calculated to upset what has for centuries been the recognized political fabric of Europe, America can remain indifferent thereto only at its own eventual cost. If it then neglects to observe that the interests of the nations crushed are likewise its own, America will be guilty of political blindness which it will later rue.

Now you could, it seems to me, have taken this view—so well substantiated by the subsequent course of events—as your point of departure, let us say, from 1913. You might then, departing from the recognition that serious troubles *were* brewing in Europe and that our own interests *were* endangered, have seen to it that this country provided itself right then and there with something in the way of an armed establishment, so that our word would carry some weight and be listened to in the councils of the powers. When war broke out, you could have ignored the nonsensical timidities of technical neutrality and used our influence to achieve the earliest possible termination of a war that nobody could really win. Admittedly, if there were any possibility of this, it was in the first months of the war, and we would have had to be armed. If this had not succeeded, then you would have had to carry on through the war, exercising what moderating influence you could, avoiding friction with the belligerents on minor matters, holding your power in reserve for the things that counted. And if you finally had to intervene to save the British from final defeat (which I am quite prepared to accept as a valid ground for intervention), then you could have gone in frankly for the avowed purpose both of doing this and of ending the war as rapidly as possible; you could have refrained from moralistic slogans, refrained from picturing your effort as a crusade, kept open your lines of negotiation to the enemy, declined to break up his empires and overthrow his political system, avoided commitments to the extremist war aims of your allies, retained your freedom of action, exploited your bargaining power flexibly with a view to bringing its full weight to bear at the crucial moments in order to achieve the termination of hostilities with a minimum prejudice to the future stability of the Continent.

All these things, as I say, you might conceivably have done. If you ask me, "Can you guarantee that this would have produced a better outcome and a happier future?" my answer is, "Of course not." I can say only that I fail to see how it could have produced a much worse one. And I can say that it would have been a conceptual framework more closely related to the realities of the world we live in and that in the long run—in the law of averages—conduct realistically motivated is likely to be more effective than conduct unrealistically motivated.

But I think I hear one great, and even indignant, objection to what I have suggested; and I must speak to it before I close. People will say to me: You know that what you have suggested was totally impossible from the standpoint of public opinion; that people in general had no idea that our interests were affected by what was going on in Europe in 1913; that they would never have dreamed of spending real money for armaments in time of peace; that they would never have gone into a war deliberately, as a result of cold calculation about the balance of power elsewhere; that they would have made war only upon direct provocation; that they could never have been brought to forgive such provocation and to refrain from pressing such a war to its final conclusion. And you know that they would not have been happy unless they had been able to clothe their military effort in the language of idealism and to persuade themselves that anything so important as Americans fighting on foreign soil had to end with a basic alteration of the terms of life among nations and a settlement of this business for once and for all. You—these people will say to me—hold yourself out as a realist, and yet none of these things you are talking about were even ever within the realm of practical possibility from the standpoint of domestic realities in our own country.

I have no quarrel with this argument. I am even going to concede it. I do think that political leaders might have made greater efforts than they did, from time to time, to inform themselves and to tell people the true facts, and I think people might even have understood them and been grateful to them if they had. But let us let that go and say that basically the argument is sound. I still have one thing to say about it.

I am not talking here about the behavior of Woodrow Wilson or Colonel House or Robert Lansing. I am talking about the behavior of the United States of America. History does not forgive us our national mistakes because they are explicable in terms of our domestic politics. If you say that mistakes of the past were unavoidable because of our domestic predilections and habits of thought, you are saying that what stopped us from being more effective than we were was democracy, as practiced in this country. And, if that is true, let us recognize it and measure the full seriousness of it—and find something to do about it. A nation which excuses its own failures by the sacred untouchableness of its own habits can excuse itself into complete disaster. I said in the first of these lectures that the margin in which it is given to us to commit blunders has been drastically narrowed in the last fifty years. If it was the workings of our democracy that were inadequate in the past, let us say so. Whoever thinks the future is going to be easier than the past is certainly mad. And the system under which we are going to have to continue to conduct foreign policy is, I hope and pray, the system of democracy.

V

WORLD WAR II

✻

THE Cambridge historian, Herbert Butterfield, recently wrote: "Behind the great conflicts of mankind is a terrible human predicament which lies at the heart of the story: . . . Contemporaries fail to see the predicament or refuse to recognize its genuineness so that our knowledge of it comes from later analysis. It is only with the progress of historical science on a particular subject that men come really to recognize that there was a terrible knot almost beyond the ingenuity of man to untie."[1]

I do not suppose that this was any more true of World War II than of any other great conflict. But the fact remains that it was a war poorly understood by the peoples who fought it on the democratic side, and particularly ourselves; and I am sure that this lack of understanding of what was involved in the conflict itself has much to do with the great bewilderment and trouble we seem now to be experiencing in our attempts to adjust ourselves to the situation it left in its train.

It occurs to me that perhaps the most helpful thing to understand about this recent war is the extent to which it was prejudiced, as a military encounter, before it was begun—the extent to which, you might say, it was not fully winnable.

Let me explain how this was. Before the war began the overwhelming portion of the world's armed strength in land forces and air forces had accumulated in the hands of three political entities—Nazi Germany, Soviet Russia, and Imperial Japan. All these entities were deeply and dangerously hostile to the

1. *The Review of Politics*, XII (April, 1950), 151–52.

74

Western democracies. As things stood in the late thirties, if these three powers were to combine their efforts and stick together in a military enterprise, the remaining Western nations plainly had no hope of defeating them on the land mass of Europe and Asia, with the armaments at hand or even those in prospect. In Europe and Asia, Western democracy had become militarily outclassed. The world balance of power had turned decisively against it.

I am not claiming that this was perceived, or would have been easy to perceive, by Western statesmen. But I believe it was a reality. And, as such, it plainly limited the actual prospects for the West, if war were to come. Of the three totalitarian powers, Japan was the only one which could conceivably be defeated by the democracies without invoking for this purpose the aid of one of the other totalitarian powers. In the case of Germany and Russia, circumstances were bitter. Together, they could not be defeated at all. Individually, either of them could be defeated only if the democracies had the collaboration of the other.

But such collaboration, if permitted to proceed to the point of complete victory, would mean the relative strengthening of the collaborating power and its eventual appearance as a greedy and implacable claimant at the peace table. Not only that: any war in which one of these two powers was fighting on the side of the democracies could scarcely be fought to a complete and successful finish without placing the collaborating totalitarian power in occupation of large parts of eastern Europe simply by virtue of the sweep of military operations.

As things stood in 1939, therefore, the Western democracies were already under the handicap of being militarily the weaker party. They could hardly have expected to avoid paying the price. Theirs were no longer the choices of strength. The cards were so stacked against them that any complete, unsullied democratic victory in a new world war was practically impossible to foresee.

Now it may be asked, from the vantage point of hindsight, whether, if this was the case, Western statesmen would not have been wiser in the years prior to hostilities to have shaped their policies in such a way as to embroil the totalitarian powers with one another in order that they might exhaust themselves and leave the security of the Western democracies undiminished. This is of course precisely what Soviet propaganda has charged Western statesmen with doing in the thirties, and indeed some of their actions were so ambiguous and ill advised as to seem to lend substance to the charge. Actually, it would be flattering to the vigor and incisiveness of Western policy in those unhappy years of the late thirties if we could believe that it was capable of such desperate and Machiavellian undertakings. I personally can find no evidence that any substantial body of responsible opinion in any of the Western countries really wished for war at all at that time—even one between Russia and Germany. It was plain that a war between the Nazis and the Russian Communists could take place only over the prostrate bodies of the small states of eastern Europe. And, notwithstanding the tragedy of Munich, the extinction of the independence of these eastern European states was something no one wished for. If other evidence of this were lacking, one had the bald fact that it was, after all, the issue of the independence of Poland for which the French and British finally went to war in 1939.

The fact is that a policy aimed deliberately at the embroilment of the totalitarian powers against each other was, for subjective reasons, never really a practical alternative for democratic statesmen. People who wish well for the democratic idea can find in that fact a source of hope or despair, depending on how they look at it. And as the shades of war closed down over Europe in the summer of 1939, the dilemma of Western statesmen, as we now see it in retrospect, was clear and inescapable. There was no prospect for victory over Germany, unless it were with the help of Russia. But for such help, even if it were forthcoming, the Western democracies would have to pay heavily in the military consequences of the war and in the demands that would be raised at the peace table. Their military purposes, in other words, were mortgaged in advance. They might be achieved, as far as Germany was concerned; but there would be a heavy political charge against them. This was not, incidentally, merely a matter of collaboration with Soviet Russia. The tortured compromises the democracies were destined eventually to make with Vichy and with Franco Spain and elsewhere were all part of this pattern. They were part of the price of Western military weakness.

It is important that these things be recognized; for when we look at the problem of Western powers in this light, bearing in mind the unpromising nature of the military undertaking on which they were embarking in 1939, we begin to wonder whether the great mistakes of Western statesmen in connection with this world war were really those of the wartime period at all—whether they were not rather the earlier mistakes, or perhaps we ought to say earlier "circumstances"— which had permitted the development of a situation so grievously and fatefully "loaded" against Western interests. This is of course the problem of the deeper origins of the war; and I think we have no choice but to face it, for the thought at once suggests itself that the best way to win so inauspicious a war might have been to find some way in which one would not have had to fight it at all. By September, 1939, it was of course too late for this. By that time the French and British had no choice, any more than we had in the Pacific in the days following Pearl Harbor. But was there a time when it was *not* too late?

The question as to what Western statesmen might have done

to avoid World War II is not an easy one. It is a little disconcerting to find respectable scholars, such as the French historian Bainville, claiming as early as 1920 to see a peculiar logic in the situation flowing from World War I and predicting quite accurately, on the basis of this logic, the general course of events up to and including the outbreak of World War II. It is disconcerting because it leads you to ask whether World War II was not perhaps implicit in the outcome of World War I; in the fact that England and France had been injured and weakened far more deeply than they knew in that first encounter; in the fact that Austria-Hungary and Russia were both lost for the maintenance of European stability, Austria-Hungary because she had disappeared entirely, Russia because her energies and resources had been captured by people violently hostile to capitalist democracy in general; and in the fact that the Germans—frustrated, impoverished, stung with defeat, uncertain in the breakdown of their traditional institutions—were nevertheless left as the only great united people in Central Europe. Looking at these things, it is easy to conclude that World War II just could not help but develop, that it was nothing more than the inevitable aftermath of World War I. You then start poking back into the origins of the earlier war to discover the real sources of the instability of our time. And from this standpoint it is only a step to absolving the Western statesmen of the twenties and thirties of all responsibility for the second war and to regarding them exclusively as the actors in a tragedy beyond their making or repair.

This is of course an extremism. Statesmen, it is true, generally inherit from their predecessors predicaments and dilemmas to which they can see no complete solutions; their ability to improve situations by action over the short term is often quite genuinely limited; but over the long term (and two decades is a respectable length of time) there are always some choices at their disposal. I think it fair to say that World War

I was a genuine tragedy which left the Western world much worse off afterward than it had been before and significantly narrowed the choices of Western statesmen in the postwar period; but it did not eliminate those choices entirely. There were, in other words, still things that "could have been done" and which we may assume would at least have been helpful and have had greater possibilities of preventing further tragedy than the things that were done. In so far as we are talking about Germany, there are two such things that strike me as of obvious importance, and in both of them we Americans could, had we wished, have taken a considerable part. First, we could have tried to give greater understanding, support, and encouragement to the moderate forces in the Weimar Republic. And if that did not succeed in preventing the rise of naziism, then we could have taken a stiffer and more resolute attitude against Hitler's earlier encroachments and provocations.

It is the last of these two possibilities, that of a stronger stand against Hitler at an earlier date, that has received most prominence in Western thought and has constituted the source of most reproaches to democratic statesmanship between the wars. Unquestionably, such a policy might have enforced a greater circumspection on the Nazi regime and caused it to proceed more slowly with the actualization of its timetable. From this standpoint, firmness at the time of the reoccupation of the Rhineland in 1936 would probably have yielded even better results than firmness at the time of Munich. But I wonder whether we do not tend to exaggerate the relative importance of this question of stopping Hitler once he was in power, as compared with the importance of seeing to it that a person of his ilk should not come into power at all in a great Western country. It was a defeat for the West, of course, that Hitler was able to consolidate his power and be successful in the years 1933–39. But actually the West had suffered an even greater defeat on the day when the German people found itself in such a frame of mind that it could, without great resistance or remonstrance, accept a Hitler as its leader and master.

A stiffer attitude on the part of the Western democracies might, it is true, have resulted in Hitler's overthrow and his replacement by a less obnoxious regime before war could come; in fact, there is evidence that a revolt might well have been attempted had the British and French had the perceptiveness to stand firm at the time of Munich. But great uncertainties lay along this path. The hypnotic charm of naziism was already strong upon the German people. If anyone had overthrown Hitler, presumably it would have been the generals. Whether they would have been able to control the situation subsequently, to lay the ghost not only of naziism but of German aggressiveness in general, and to adjust peaceably their relations with the West, is not certain. The great misfortune of the West, I suspect, was not Hitler but the weakness of German society which made possible his triumph. And it is this which takes us back to this question of the attitude of the Western democracies toward the Weimar Republic.

Events have moved so fast that we have almost lost sight of this intensely interesting period in German history—the period before 1933, with its amazing cultural and intellectual flowering, so full of hope and yet so close to despair. In the decade of the twenties Berlin was the most alive of the capitals of Europe, and things were taking place there from which the Western democracies might have derived profit and instruction. It is true that the peace treaty we Americans concluded with Wiemar Germany was nonpunitive. Americans cannot be justly charged with any political offensiveness toward the new Germany. We even financed her lavishly, though foolishly. But what I am thinking of pertained not just to us but to the Western democracies in general, and it was something more than political or financial: it was a general attitude of distaste and suspicion, intermingled with a sort of social snobbery so

grotesque that as late as 1927 a German could still be pro-
hibited from using the golf links at Geneva, the seat of the
League of Nations. We did nothing to harm Weimar Germany;
but we left it very much to its own devices. There are times
when that is a good policy toward another country. But I fear
that this was not one of those times. Here, in any case, were
lost opportunities; and it is significant that they lay as much
in the cultural and intellectual as in the political field.

Now a word about Russia, the second totalitarian party.
Was there nothing we could have done, prior to 1939, to keep
this great country out of the camp of our adversaries? I am
sorry that we cannot devote an entire lecture to this subject,
for it is an interesting one and close to my heart. I do not feel
that we in this country always conducted ourselves in the
manner best calculated to reduce the dimensions of the Soviet
threat. I think we might have done more to win the respect, if
not the liking, of the Russian Communists; and the respect of
your enemies—as we are apt sometimes to forget—is nothing
to be sneezed at. But I know of little that we could have done
to alter basically the political personality of the Bolshevik
leadership or to moderate the violent preconceptions against
Western democracy on which it was reared and with which it
came into power. These things had deep psychological roots,
lying in specifically Russian phenomena. Whether the capitalist democracies of the West had done things prior to 1917
to deserve this burning hostility, I do not know. But I am
sure that, once developed, it was hardly to be altered by anything the West might do directly; and the best reaction to it
on our part would have been at all times an attitude of great
reserve, consistency, and dignity.

As for Japan, the problem of whether she had also to be
ranged against us in war in the early 1940's was of course primarily our problem, not that of the French and British. I
would wish that we could skip it entirely for purposes of this

discussion; for it is a tremendous subject in itself, relatively remote from the causes of the war in Europe, and not easy to treat in a few words. But the fact of our simultaneous involvement with Japan and Germany was so important an element in the course and outcome of the war that I think one cannot simply pass the question by.

To discuss this problem at all adequately would be to discuss the entire sequence of American-Japanese relations over the half-century preceding the outbreak of war in the Pacific; and that we obviously cannot do here. To this we must add the disturbing fact that there can never be any certainty about these post mortems on history. It does seem plain that, as the earlier decades and years of this century went by and the hour of Pearl Harbor approached, the choices of American statesmen that held promise of averting a war with Japan became narrower and narrower, and no one can be sure, I suppose, that anything we might have done or failed to do in the final years and months before the Japanese attack could really have forestalled the final outcome. If there were happier possibilities, they were surely more abundant in the more distant past, when our allotment of time was more generous and our area of diplomatic maneuver greater. But whether such possibilities really existed must remain a matter of opinion. My own feeling, for whatever it is worth, is that a policy carefully and realistically aimed at the avoidance of a war with Japan and less encumbered with other motives would certainly have produced a line of action considerably different from that which we actually pursued and would presumably have led to quite different results.

But I think it is enough for us to record that here again, as in the European theater, if there were ways in which this war might have been avoided altogether, they were probably ways that did relate to the more distant past: to a period when people were not thinking about war at all and had no idea that the things they were doing or failing to do were creating for them this tremendous predicament of the future.

So we are back again to our fundamental fact that by the year 1939 affairs were really quite inauspicious for the Western democracies. The situation which they had allowed to arise was one for which there were no complete cures. Whether they realized it or not, the war could be for them, in the deeper sense, at best a war of defense: a war that might bring immediate survival but could scarcely bring an improvement in the stability of the world they lived in, and certainly not the advance of any of the more positive and constructive purposes of democracy. When this is borne in mind, the great decisions of the war years themselves appear for the most part in a more charitable light.

The first of these great decisions which deserves mention seems to me to have been our own decision—if we may call it that—not to enter the European war until the Germans declared war upon us. This was of course comparable to our behavior in World War I, when we refrained from entering until an overt German action, namely, the declaration of unrestricted submarine warfare, brought us in. And what seems to me most interesting about our conduct in each of these cases is the marked change in our emotional attitude toward the struggle itself, once we had become formally involved in it. Theoretically, if the issues involved in the European struggle were really as vital to us as we persuaded ourselves they were in the years 1942–45, they were surely no less important from 1939 to 1941. Actually, in that earlier period, before the German attack on Russia, the cause of the British and French could really be called the cause of freedom and democracy, for very little else was involved on the Western side; whereas later, when we did discover that our vital stake in the anti-German cause warranted great military sacrifice on our part, it was at a time when that cause had been rendered ambiguous, as anything more than a defensive undertaking, by the participation of the U.S.S.R. on the side of the democracies.

Now I mention this, because, making all due allowance for the deliberateness of the opinion-forming process in a democracy, it does look as though the real source of the emotional fervor which we Americans are able to put into a war lies less in any objective understanding of the wider issues involved than in a profound irritation over the fact that other people have finally provoked us to the point where we had no alternative but to take up arms. This lends to the democratic war effort a basically punitive note, rather than one of expediency. I mention this because, if there is anything in this thought, it goes far to explain the difficulty we have in employing force for rational and restricted purposes rather than for purposes which are emotional and to which it is hard to find a rational limit.

Once we had come into the European war, and granted the heavy military handicaps with which the Western powers were then confronted in that theater, the decisions taken throughout the remainder of the war years were those of harried, overworked men, operating in the vortex of a series of tremendous pressures, military and otherwise, which we today find it difficult to remember or to imagine. I think that some injustice is being done both to the men in question and to the cause of historical understanding by the latter-day interpretations which regard specific decisions of the wartime years as the source of all our present difficulties. The most vociferous charges of wartime mistakes relate primarily to our dealings with the U.S.S.R., and particularly to the wartime conferences of Moscow, Teheran, and Yalta. As one who was very unhappy about these conferences at the time they were taking place and very worried lest they lead to false hopes and misunderstandings, I may perhaps be permitted to say that I think their importance has recently been considerably overrated. If it cannot be said that the Western democracies gained very much from these talks with the Russians, it would also be incorrect to say that they gave very much away. The establishment of Soviet military power in eastern Europe and the entry of Soviet forces into Manchuria was not the result of these talks; it was the result of the military operations during the concluding phases of the war. There was nothing the Western democracies could have done to prevent the Russians from entering these areas except to get there first, and this they were not in a position to do. The implication that Soviet forces would not have gone into Manchuria if Roosevelt had not arrived at the Yalta understanding with Stalin is surely nonsense. Nothing could have stopped the Russians from participating in the final phases of the Pacific war, in order to be in at the kill and to profit by an opportunity to gain objectives they had been seeking for half a century.

It is similarly incorrect to portray the Yalta agreement as a terrible betrayal of Nationalist China. The agreement was that we should recommend certain things to the Chinese government. The leaders of that government were not averse to these things at the time. They had asked us, long before Yalta, to help them to arrange their affairs with the Soviet government. They later expressed themselves as well satisfied with what we had done. And in the subsequent negotiations which they themselves conducted independently with the Russians and which actually constituted the controlling arrangements for the future of Manchuria, they went in some respects further in the way of concessions to the Soviet Union than anything that had been agreed upon at Yalta and recommended to them by us. They did this despite the fact that they were specifically warned by us that in doing so they were acting on their own responsibility and not at our recommendation.

The worst that can fairly be said about the wartime conferences from the practical standpoint, therefore, is that they were somewhat redundant and led to a certain number of false hopes here and elsewhere. But we must remember, in this connection, that these conferences had a distinct value as practical demonstrations of our readiness and eagerness to establish better relations with the Soviet regime and of the difficulties we encountered in our effort to do so. Like other evidences of patience and good will, they were important for the record. Had we not gone into them, it is my guess that we would still be hearing reproachful voices saying: "You claim that cooperation with Russia is not possible. How do you know? You never even tried."

A more substantial charge against our wartime policy toward Russia, although one we hear less about, is that which relates to the continuation of lend-lease during the latter period of the war, and specifically subsequent to midsummer of 1944. By that time, as you will recall, Russia's own territory had been freed of the enemy; our own talking position vis-à-vis the Russians had been considerably improved by the creation of a successful second front; and from there on out whatever the Russian forces did was bound to have important political consequences for European peoples other than the Germans—consequences which went far beyond the mere defeat of Germany. I think it can be well argued that there was no adequate justification for refusing to give any attention to these developing political problems and for continuing a program of lavish and almost indiscriminate aid to the Soviet Union at a time when there was increasing reason to doubt whether her purposes in eastern Europe, aside from the defeat of Germany, would be ones which we Americans could approve and sponsor.

But in all these matters we must bear in mind both the overriding compulsion of military necessity under which our statesmen were working and also the depth of their conviction that one had no choice but to gamble on the possibility that

Soviet suspicions might be broken down and Soviet collaboration won for the postwar period, if there were to be any hope of permanent peace. Many of us who were familiar with Russian matters were impatient with this line of thought at the time, because we knew how poor were the chances of success, and we saw no reason why a Western world which kept its nerves, its good humor, and a due measure of military preparedness should not continue indefinitely to live in the same world with the power of the Kremlin without flying to either of the extremes of political intimacy or war. In the light of what has occurred subsequently, I can see that our view, too, was not fully rounded. We were right about the nature of Soviet power; but we were wrong about the ability of American democracy at this stage in its history to bear for long a situation full of instability, inconvenience, and military danger. Perhaps Harry Hopkins and F. D. R. had more reason than we then supposed to believe that everything depended on the possibility of changing the attitude of the Soviet regime. But, if so, this is then only an indication that the dilemma was crueler than any of us really appreciated, and the crisis of our time one of such profundity that even the vast dislocations of World War II were only a partial symptom of it.

And there is no reason to suppose that, had we behaved differently either with respect to lend-lease or with respect to the wartime conferences, the outcome of military events in Europe would have been greatly different than it was. We might have wasted less money and material than we did. We might have arrived in the center of Europe slightly sooner and less encumbered with obligations to our Soviet allies. The postwar line of division between East and West might have lain somewhat farther east than it does today, and that would certainly be a relief to everyone concerned. But we were still up against the basic dilemma that Hitler was a man with whom a compromise peace was impracticable and unthinkable and that, while "unconditional surrender" was probably not a wise thing to talk a lot about and make into a wartime slogan, in reality there was no promising alternative but to pursue this unhappy struggle to its bitter end, whether you were acting in agreement with your Russian allies or whether you were not; and this meant that sooner or later you would end on some sort of a line in eastern or Central Europe, probably more central than eastern, with ourselves on one side and Soviet forces on the other, and with the understanding between us just about what it has proved to be in these six years since the termination of hostilities.

Remembering these things, I think we are justified in asking whether the greatest mistakes of World War II were really these tortured and hard-pressed decisions which defined military operations and gave shape to inter-Allied relations in the stress of military operations—whether they were really, in other words, the errors of decision on the part of a few highly placed individuals—whether they were not rather the deeper mistakes of understanding and attitude on the part of our society in general with respect to a military venture in which we were engaged. First of all, there was the failure to remember the essentially and inescapably defensive nature of this particular war, as one in which we in the West were at first the weaker party, capable of achieving only a portion of our aim and of achieving that portion only in collaboration with a totalitarian adversary and at a price. This failure stemmed from our general ignorance of the historical processes of our age and particularly from our lack of attention to the power realities involved in given situations.

But beyond that, it seems to me, there lay a deeper failure of understanding, a failure to appreciate the limitations of war in general—any war—as a vehicle for the achievement of the objectives of the democratic state. This is the question of the proper relationship of such things as force and coercion to the purposes of democracy. That they have a place in the international as well as the domestic functioning of democracy I would be the last to deny. That will continue to be true until the world is an entirely different world from what we have known it to be throughout our national history. But I would submit that we will continue to harm our own interests almost as much as we benefit them if we continue to employ the instruments of coercion in the international field without a better national understanding of their significance and possibilities. It is essential to recognize that the maiming and killing of men and the destruction of human shelters and other installations, however necessary it may be for other reasons, cannot in itself make a positive contribution to any democratic purpose. It can be the regrettable alternative to similar destruction in our own country or the killing of our own people. It can conceivably protect values which it is necessary to protect and which can be protected in no other way. Occasionally, if used with forethought and circumspection and restraint, it may trade the lesser violence for the greater and impel the stream of human events into channels which will be more hopeful ones than it would otherwise have taken. But, basically, the democratic purpose does not prosper when a man dies or a building collapses or an enemy force retreats. It may be hard for it to prosper *unless* these things happen, and in that lies the entire justification for the use of force at all as a weapon of national policy. But the actual prospering occurs only when something happens in a man's mind that increases his enlightenment and the consciousness of his real relation to other people—something that makes him aware that, whenever the dignity of another man is offended, his own dignity, as a man among men, is thereby reduced. And this is why the destructive process of war must always be accompanied by, or made subsidiary to, a different sort of undertaking aimed at widening the horizons and changing the motives of men and should never be thought of in itself as a proper vehicle for hopes and enthusiasms and dreams of world improvement.

Force, like peace, is not an abstraction; it cannot be understood or dealt with as a concept outside of the given framework of purpose and method. If this were better understood, there could be neither the sweeping moral rejection of international violence which bedevils so many Americans in times of peace nor the helpless abandonment to its compulsions and its inner momentum which characterizes so many of us in times of war.

It is hard for me to say how different would have been our situation today had our public opinion and the mental outlook of our leading persons comprised a comprehension of these realities throughout the entire period of the thirties and forties which we associate with World War II. It is easy to imagine that war might never have come upon us in the form that it did had this been the case. Or, perhaps, even if it had come upon us, we might have been prepared to enter it sooner and in greater force, and thus have been able to end it in a way more favorable to the interests of moderation and stability in world affairs. But these are only conjectures. The historian can never prove that a better comprehension of realities would have prevented any specific calamity or obviated any of the major human predicaments. He can only say that in the law of averages it should have helped.

At the very worst, we can be sure that, had we understood better the elements of our predicament during World War II, we would be calmer and more united and less irritated with one another today in this country, for we would have been better prepared for the things that have happened since 1945 and less inclined to mistake them for the product of somebody else's stupidity or bad faith. But actually it is my belief, which I cannot prove, that the benefits would have gone much farther than this. The possibilities which lie in human understanding, like those that lie in darkness and ignorance, are seldom hypothetically demonstrable; but sometimes they are surprising.

VI

DIPLOMACY IN THE MODERN WORLD

✢

THESE lectures were designed as historical exercises, as contributions to the analysis of past events in the field of American diplomacy; and normally they might have been permitted to stand as such. But the background of current events against which they have been given has been so absorbing, and your own preoccupation with these events so obvious and understandable, that I know you will feel that what I have said has not been given its maximum usefulness if I do not add a word about its relevance to our problems of today.

Before I do this, there is one more thing I would like to say about the past. I fear that the impression I have given you of our past performance in the diplomatic field may have been a darker and gloomier one than is really in my mind. I ought to record, I think, my own recognition that the annals of American diplomacy in this half-century contain many positive aspects as well as negative ones. Let us remember that for us this has been a period of tremendous and most trying transition. We entered upon it with the concepts and methods of a small neutral nation. I know this approach well. I have seen it in some of the foreign offices of other countries where I have been privileged to do business on behalf of our government. It is an approach which I like and respect, and for which I must confess a certain nostalgia. It can have in it, and usually does, great quality and dignity. The Department of State as it existed at the turn of the century, and as it still was in large measure in the 1920's when I entered it, was a quaint old

91

place, with its law-office atmosphere, its cool dark corridors, its swinging doors, its brass cuspidors, its black leather rocking chairs, and the grandfather's clock in the Secretary of State's office. There was a real old-fashioned dignity and simplicity about it. It was staffed in those earlier days by professional personnel some of whom were men of great experience and competence. And it was headed more often than otherwise by Americans of genuine stature and quality.

I should be most unhappy if anything said in these lectures should seem a mark of disrespect for such men as John Hay, Elihu Root, Charles Evans Hughes, or Henry Stimson. These men embodied that pattern of integrity of mind and spirit, moderation and delicacy of character, irreproachable loyalty in personal relations, modesty of person combined with dignity of office, and kindliness and generosity in the approach to all who were weaker and more dependent, which constitutes, it seems to me, our finest contribution to the variety of the human species in this world and comes closest to embodying our national ideal and genius. They were men so measured and prudent in their judgment of others, so careful to reserve that judgment until they felt they had the facts, so well aware of the danger of inadequate evidence and hasty conclusion, that we would be making ourselves ridiculous if we were to attend their memories and the evidences of their handiwork in any other spirit.

We are another generation, and we cannot be fully the judges either of the demands which faced our elders or of the adequacy of their responses. For the performance of these men in public office I can feel only the sort of sympathy and admiration which one felt for the struggles and works of one's own father, coupled with the invariable conviction of children everywhere that there were features of the modern world which Father understood very poorly and we children understood much better. And if, today, we think we see blind spots or weak spots in their approaches to foreign policy, we would do well to remember what Gibbon said of the great Byzantine general, Belisarius: "His imperfections flowed from the contagion of the times: his virtues were his own."

But, notwithstanding all this, it is clear that there has been in the past a very significant gap between challenge and response in our conduct of foreign policy; that this gap still exists; and that, whereas fifty years ago it was not very dangerous to us, today it puts us in grave peril. We can afford no complacency about these things in the year 1951, and we have no choice but to face up unsparingly to our weaknesses.

I think you have seen quite clearly from the earlier lectures what I hold these weaknesses to be. I do not need to recapitulate them in any great detail. They are ones which relate both to machinery and to concept—both to means and to objectives.

On the question of the machinery of government, we have seen that a good deal of our trouble seems to have stemmed from the extent to which the executive has felt itself beholden to short-term trends of public opinion in the country and from what we might call the erratic and subjective nature of public reaction to foreign-policy questions. I would like to emphasize that I do not consider public reaction to foreign-policy questions to be erratic and undependable over the long term; but I think the record indicates that in the short term our public opinion, or what passes for our public opinion in the thinking of official Washington, can be easily led astray into areas of emotionalism and subjectivity which make it a poor and inadequate guide for national action.

What can we do about this?

As one who has occupied himself professionally with foreign affairs for a quarter of a century, I cannot refrain from saying that I firmly believe that we could make much more effective use of the principle of professionalism in the conduct of foreign policy; that we could, if we wished, develop a corps of professional officers superior to anything that exists or ever has existed in this field; and that, by treating these men with respect and drawing on their insight and experience, we could help ourselves considerably. However, I am quite prepared to recognize that this runs counter to strong prejudices and preconceptions in sections of our public mind, particularly in Congress and the press, and that for this reason we are probably condemned to continue relying almost exclusively on what we might call "diplomacy by dilettantism."

That being the case, we still have with us, in what is obviously a very acute form, the problem of the machinery for decision-making and for the implementation of policy in our government. Whatever else may be said about these facilities to date, it can hardly be said that they are distinguished by such things as privacy, deliberateness, or the long-term approach. The difficulties we encounter here are so plain to all of you at this moment that I shall not attempt to adumbrate them. The subject of their correction is an extremely complex one, involving many facets of governmental organization and method. There are those who feel that these difficulties can be satisfactorily disposed of within our present constitutional framework and that they are simply a question of proper personal leadership in government. There are others who doubt that the problem is soluble without constitutional reform—reform which would give us a parliamentary system more nearly like that which exists in England and most other parliamentary countries, a system in which a government falls if it loses the confidence of its parliament, and in which there is opportunity to consult the people on the great issues and at the crucial moments and to adjust governmental responsibilities in accordance with the peoples' decision.

I must say that if I had any doubts before as to whether it is this that our country requires, those doubts have been pretty well resolved in my mind by the events of the past weeks and months. I find it hard to see how we can live up to our responsibilities as a great power unless we are able to resolve, in a manner better than we have done recently, the great challenges to the soundness of government policy and to the claim of an administration to speak for the mass of the people in foreign affairs.

Here again, I am afraid, the chances of change in the direction I have indicated are so slight that we must dismiss the possibility as one that might have any particular relevance to our present problems.

This leaves us substantially with the question of concept. This is the field in which the scholar's voice can be most useful, and for which it seems to me that this examination of the past yields the most instructive results.

As you have no doubt surmised, I see the most serious fault of our past policy formulation to lie in something that I might call the legalistic-moralistic approach to international problems. This approach runs like a red skein through our foreign policy of the last fifty years. It has in it something of the old emphasis on arbitration treaties, something of the Hague Conferences and schemes for universal disarmament, something of the more ambitious American concepts of the role of international law, something of the League of Nations and the United Nations, something of the Kellogg Pact, something of the idea of a universal "Article 51" pact, something of the belief in World Law and World Government. But it is none of these, entirely. Let me try to describe it.

It is the belief that it should be possible to suppress the chaotic and dangerous aspirations of governments in the international field by the acceptance of some system of legal rules and restraints. This belief undoubtedly represents in part an attempt to transpose the Anglo-Saxon concept of individual law into the international field and to make it applicable to governments as it is applicable here at home to individuals.

It must also stem in part from the memory of the origin of our own political system—from the recollection that we were able, through acceptance of a common institutional and juridical framework, to reduce to harmless dimensions the conflicts of interest and aspiration among the original thirteen colonies and to bring them all into an ordered and peaceful relationship with one another. Remembering this, people are unable to understand that what might have been possible for the thirteen colonies in a given set of circumstances might not be possible in the wider international field.

 Not true today

It is the essence of this belief that, instead of taking the awkward conflicts of national interest and dealing with them on their merits with a view to finding the solutions least unsettling to the stability of international life, it would be better to find some formal criteria of a juridical nature by which the permissible behavior of states could be defined. There would then be judicial entities competent to measure the actions of governments against these criteria and to decide when their behavior was acceptable and when unacceptable. Behind all this, of course, lies the American assumption that the things for which other peoples in this world are apt to contend are for the most part neither creditable nor important and might justly be expected to take second place behind the desirability of an orderly world, untroubled by international violence. To the American mind, it is implausible that people should have positive aspirations, and ones that they regard as legitimate, more important to them than the peacefulness and orderliness of international life. From this standpoint, it is not apparent why other peoples should not join us in accepting the rules of the game in international politics, just as we accept such rules in the competition of sport in order that the game may not become too cruel and too destructive and may not assume an importance we did not mean it to have.

If they were to do this, the reasoning runs, then the troublesome and chaotic manifestations of the national ego could be contained and rendered either unsubstantial or subject to easy disposal by some method familiar and comprehensible to our American usage. Departing from this background, the mind of American statesmanship, stemming as it does in so large a part from the legal profession in our country, gropes with unfailing persistence for some institutional framework which would be capable of fulfilling this function.

I cannot undertake in this short lecture to deal exhaustively with this thesis or to point out all the elements of unsoundness which I feel it contains. But some of its more outstanding weaknesses are worthy of mention.

In the first place, the idea of the subordination of a large number of states to an international juridical regime, limiting their possibilities for aggression and injury to other states, implies that these are all states like our own, reasonably content with their international borders and status, at least to the extent that they would be willing to refrain from pressing for change without international agreement. Actually, this has generally been true only of a portion of international society. We tend to underestimate the violence of national maladjustments and discontents elsewhere in the world if we think that they would always appear to other people as less important than the preservation of the juridical tidiness of international life.

Second, while this concept is often associated with a revolt against nationalism, it is a curious thing that it actually tends to confer upon the concept of nationality and national sovereignty an absolute value it did not have before. The very principle of "one government, one vote," regardless of physical or political differences between states, glorifies the concept of national sovereignty and makes it the exclusive form of participation in international life. It envisages a world composed exclusively of sovereign national states with a full equality of status. In doing this, it ignores the tremendous variations in the firmness and soundness of national divisions: the fact that the origins of state borders and national personalities were in many instances fortuitous or at least poorly related to realities. It also ignores the law of change. The national state pattern is not, should not be, and cannot be a fixed and static thing. By nature, it is an unstable phenomenon in a constant state of change and flux. History has shown that the will and the capacity of individual peoples to contribute to their world environment is constantly changing. It is only logical that the organizational forms (and what else are such things as borders and governments?) should change with them. The function of a system of international relationships is not to inhibit this process of change by imposing a legal strait jacket upon it but rather to facilitate it: to ease its transitions, to temper the asperities to which it often leads, to isolate and moderate the conflicts to which it gives rise, and to see that these conflicts do not assume forms too unsettling for international life in general. But this is a task for diplomacy, in the most old-fashioned sense of the term. For this, law is too abstract, too inflexible, too hard to adjust to the demands of the unpredictable and the unexpected.

By the same token, the American concept of world law ignores those means of international offense—those means of the projection of power and coercion over other peoples—which by-pass institutional forms entirely or even exploit them against themselves: such things as ideological attack, intimidation, penetration, and disguised seizure of the institutional paraphernalia of national sovereignty. It ignores, in other words, the device of the puppet state and the set of techniques by which states can be converted into puppets with no formal violation of, or challenge to, the outward attributes of their sovereignty and their independence.

This is one of the things that have caused the peoples of the satellite countries of eastern Europe to look with a certain tinge of bitterness on the United Nations. The organization failed so completely to save them from domination by a great neighboring country, a domination no less invidious by virtue of the fact that it came into being by processes we could not call "aggression." And there is indeed some justification for their feeling, because the legalistic approach to international affairs ignores in general the international significance of political problems and the deeper sources of international instability. It assumes that civil wars will remain civil and not grow into international wars. It assumes the ability of each people to solve its own internal political problems in a manner not provocative of its international environment. It assumes that each nation will always be able to construct a government qualified to speak for it and cast its vote in the international arena and that this government will be acceptable to the rest of the international community in this capacity. It assumes, in other words, that domestic issues will not become international issues and that the world community will not be put in the position of having to make choices between rival claimants for power within the confines of the individual state.

Finally, this legalistic approach to international relations is faulty in its assumptions concerning the possibility of sanctions against offenses and violations. In general, it looks to collective action to provide such sanction against the bad behavior of states. In doing so, it forgets the limitations on the effectiveness of military coalition. It forgets that, as a circle of military associates widens in any conceivable political-military venture, the theoretical total of available military strength may increase, but only at the cost of compactness and ease of control. And the wider a coalition becomes, the more difficult it becomes to retain political unity and general agreement on the purposes and effects of what is being done. As we are seeing in the case of Korea, joint military operations against an aggressor have a different meaning for each participant and raise specific political issues for each one which are extraneous to the action in question and affect many other facets of international life. The wider the circle of military associates, the more cumbersome the problem of political control over their actions, and the more circumscribed the least common denominator of agreement. This law of diminishing returns lies so heavily on the possibilities for multilateral military action that it makes it doubtful whether the participation of smaller states can really add very much to the ability of the great powers to assure stability of international life. And this is tremendously important, for it brings us back to the realization that even under a system of world law the sanction against destructive international behavior might continue to rest basically, as it has in the past, on the alliances and relationships among the great powers themselves. There might be a state, or perhaps more than one state, which all the rest of the world community together could not successfully coerce into following a line of action to which it was violently averse. And if this is true, where are we? It seems to me that we are right back in the realm of the forgotten art of diplomacy from which we have spent fifty years trying to escape.

These, then, are some of the theoretical deficiencies that appear to me to be inherent in the legalistic approach to international affairs. But there is a greater deficiency still that I should like to mention before I close. That is the inevitable association of legalistic ideas with moralistic ones: the carrying-over into the affairs of states of the concepts of right and wrong, the assumption that state behavior is a fit subject for moral judgment. Whoever says there is a law must of course be indignant against the lawbreaker and feel a moral superiority to him. And when such indignation spills over into military contest, it knows no bounds short of the reduction of the lawbreaker to the point of complete submissiveness—namely, unconditional surrender. It is a curious thing, but it is true, that the legalistic approach to world affairs, rooted as it unquestionably is in a desire to do away with war and violence, makes violence more enduring, more terrible, and more destructive to political stability than did the older motives of national interest. A war fought in the name of high moral principle finds no early end short of some form of total domination.

In this way, we see that the legalistic approach to international problems is closely identified with the concept of total war and total victory, and the manifestations of the one spill over only too easily into the manifestations of the other. And the concept of total war is something we would all do well to think about a little in these troubled times. This is a relatively new concept, in Western civilization at any rate. It did not really appear on the scene until World War I. It characterized both of these great world wars, and both of them—as I have pointed out—were followed by great instability and disillusionment. But it is not only a question now of the desirability of this concept; it is a question of its feasibility. Actually, I wonder whether even in the past total victory was not really an illusion from the standpoint of the victors. In a sense, there is not total victory short of genocide, unless it be a victory over the minds of men. But the total military victories are rarely victories over the minds of men. And we now face the fact that it is very questionable whether in a new global conflict there could ever be any such thing as total *military* victory. I personally do not believe that there could. There might be a great weakening of the armed forces of one side or another, but I think it out of the question that there should be such a thing as a general and formal submission of the national will on either side. The attempt to achieve this unattainable goal, however, could wreak upon civilization another set of injuries fully as serious as those caused by

World War I or World War II, and I leave it to you to answer the question as to how civilization could survive them.

It was asserted not long ago by a prominent American that "war's very object is victory" and that "in war there can be no substitute for victory." Perhaps the confusion here lies in what is meant by the term "victory." Perhaps the term is actually misplaced. Perhaps there can be such a thing as "victory" in a battle, whereas in war there can be only the achievement or nonachievement of your objectives. In the old days, wartime objectives were generally limited and practical ones, and it was common to measure the success of your military operations by the extent to which they brought you closer to your objectives. But where your objectives are moral and ideological ones and run to changing the attitudes and traditions of an entire people or the personality of a regime, then victory is probably something not to be achieved entirely by military means or indeed in any short space of time at all; and perhaps that is the source of our confusion.

In any case, I am frank to say that I think there is no more dangerous delusion, none that has done us a greater disservice in the past or that threatens to do us a greater disservice in the future, than the concept of total victory. And I fear that it springs in large measure from the basic faults in the approach to international affairs which I have been discussing here. If we are to get away from it, this will not mean that we shall have to abandon our respect for international law, or our hopes for its future usefulness as the gentle civilizer of events which I mentioned in one of the earlier lectures. Nor will it mean that we have to go in for anything that can properly be termed "appeasement"—if one may use a word so cheapened and deflated by the abuse to which it has been recently subjected. But it will mean the emergence of a new attitude among us toward many things outside our borders that are irritating and unpleasant today—an attitude more like that of the doctor toward those physical phenomena in the human body that are neither pleasing nor fortunate—an attitude of detachment and soberness and readiness to reserve judgment. It will mean that we will have the modesty to admit that our own national interest is all that we are really capable of knowing and understanding—and the courage to recognize that if our own purposes and undertakings here at home are decent ones, unsullied by arrogance or hostility toward other people or delusions of superiority, then the pursuit of our national interest can never fail to be conducive to a better world. This concept is less ambitious and less inviting in its immediate prospects than those to which we have so often inclined, and less pleasing to our image of ourselves. To many it may seem to smack of cynicism and reaction. I cannot share these doubts. Whatever is realistic in concept, and founded in an endeavor to see both ourselves and others as we really are, cannot be illiberal.

PART II

THE SOURCES OF SOVIET CONDUCT*

✧

I

THE political personality of Soviet power as we know it today is the product of ideology and circumstances: ideology inherited by the present Soviet leaders from the movement in which they had their political origin, and circumstances of the power which they now have exercised for nearly three decades in Russia. There can be few tasks of psychological analysis more difficult than to try to trace the interaction of these two forces and the relative role of each in the determination of official Soviet conduct. Yet the attempt must be made if that conduct is to be understood and effectively countered.

It is difficult to summarize the set of ideological concepts with which the Soviet leaders came into power. Marxian ideology, in its Russian-Communist projection, has always been in process of subtle evolution. The materials on which it bases itself are extensive and complex. But the outstanding features of Communist thought as it existed in 1916 may perhaps be summarized as follows: (*a*) that the central factor in the life of man, the fact which determines the character of public life and the "physiognomy of society," is the system by which material goods are produced and exchanged; (*b*) that the capitalist system of production is a nefarious one which inevitably leads to the exploitation of the working class by the capital-owning class and is incapable of developing adequately the economic resources of society or of distributing

* Reprinted, by permission of the editor, from *Foreign Affairs*, XXV, No. 4 (July, 1947), 566–82. Copyright 1947 by Council on Foreign Relations, Inc.

fairly the material goods produced by human labor; (c) that capitalism contains the seeds of its own destruction and must, in view of the inability of the capital-owning class to adjust itself to economic change, result eventually and inescapably in a revolutionary transfer of power to the working class; and (d) that imperialism, the final phase of capitalism, leads directly to war and revolution.

The rest may be outlined in Lenin's own words: "Unevenness of economic and political development is the inflexible law of capitalism. It follows from this that the victory of Socialism may come originally in a few capitalist countries or even in a single capitalist country. The victorious proletariat of that country, having expropriated the capitalists and having organized Socialist production at home, would rise against the remaining capitalist world, drawing to itself in the process the oppressed classes of other countries."[1] It must be noted that there was no assumption that capitalism would perish without proletarian revolution. A final push was needed from a revolutionary proletariat movement in order to tip over the tottering structure. But it was regarded as inevitable that sooner or later that push be given.

For fifty years prior to the outbreak of the Revolution, this pattern of thought had exercised great fascination for the members of the Russian revolutionary movement. Frustrated, discontented, hopeless of finding self-expression—or too impatient to seek it—in the confining limits of the Tsarist political system, yet lacking wide popular support for their choice of bloody revolution as a means of social betterment, these revolutionists found in Marxist theory a highly convenient rationalization for their own instinctive desires. It afforded pseudo-scientific justification for their impatience, for their categoric denial of all value in the Tsarist system, for their

1. *Concerning the Slogans of the United States of Europe, August 1915* (Official Soviet edition of Lenin's works).

yearning for power and revenge and for their inclination to cut corners in the pursuit of it. It is therefore no wonder that they had come to believe implicitly in the truth and soundness of the Marxian-Leninist teachings, so congenial to their own impulses and emotions. Their sincerity need not be impunged. This is a phenomenon as old as human nature itself. It has never been more aptly described than by Edward Gibbon, who wrote in *The Decline and Fall of the Roman Empire:* "From enthusiasm to imposture the step is perilous and slippery; the demon of Socrates affords a memorable instance how a wise man may deceive himself; how a good man may deceive others, how the conscience may slumber in a mixed and middle state between self-illusion and voluntary fraud." And it was with this set of conceptions that the members of the Bolshevik Party entered into power.

Now it must be noted that through all the years of preparation for revolution, the attention of these men, as indeed of Marx himself, had been centered less on the future form which Socialism[2] would take than on the necessary overthrow of rival power which, in their view, had to precede the introduction of Socialism. Their views, therefore, on the positive program to be put into effect, once power was attained, were for the most part nebulous, visionary and impractical. Beyond the nationalization of industry and the expropriation of large private capital holdings there was no agreed program. The treatment of the peasantry, which according to the Marxist formulation was not of the proletariat, had always been a vague spot in the pattern of Communist thought; and it remained an object of controversy and vacillation for the first ten years of Communist power.

The circumstances of the immediate post-Revolution period—the existence in Russia of civil war and foreign inter-

2. Here and elsewhere in this paper "Socialism" refers to Marxist or Leninist Communism, not to liberal Socialism of the Second International variety.

vention, together with the obvious fact that the Communists represented only a tiny minority of the Russian people—made the establishment of dictatorial power a necessity. The experiment with "war Communism" and the abrupt attempt to eliminate private production and trade had unfortunate economic consequences and caused further bitterness against the new revolutionary regime. While the temporary relaxation of the effort to communize Russia, represented by the New Economic Policy, alleviated some of this economic distress and thereby served its purpose, it also made it evident that the "capitalistic sector of society" was still prepared to profit at once from any relaxation of governmental pressure, and would, if permitted to continue to exist, always constitute a powerful opposing element to the Soviet regime and a serious rival for influence in the country. Somewhat the same situation prevailed with respect to the individual peasant who, in his own small way, was also a private producer.

Lenin, had he lived, might have proved a great enough man to reconcile these conflicting forces to the ultimate benefit of Russian society, though this is questionable. But be that as it may, Stalin, and those whom he led in the struggle for succession to Lenin's position of leadership, were not the men to tolerate rival political forces in the sphere of power which they coveted. Their sense of insecurity was too great. Their particular brand of fanaticism, unmodified by any of the Anglo-Saxon traditions of compromise, was too fierce and too jealous to envisage any permanent sharing of power. From the Russian-Asiatic world out of which they had emerged they carried with them a skepticism as to the possibilities of permanent and peaceful coexistence of rival forces. Easily persuaded of their own doctrinaire "rightness," they insisted on the submission or destruction of all competing power. Outside of the Communist Party, Russian society was to have no rigidity. There were to be no forms of collective human activity or association which would not be dominated by the Party. No other force in Russian society was to be permitted to achieve vitality or integrity. Only the Party was to have structure. All else was to be an amorphous mass.

And within the Party the same principle was to apply. The mass of Party members might go through the motions of election, deliberation, decision and action; but in these motions they were to be animated not by their own individual wills but by the awesome breath of the Party leadership and the overbrooding presence of "the world."

Let it be stressed again that subjectively these men probably did not seek absolutism for its own sake. They doubtless believed—and found it easy to believe—that they alone knew what was good for society and that they would accomplish that good once their power was secure and unchallengeable. But in seeking that security of their own rule they were prepared to recognize no restrictions, either of God or man, on the character of their methods. And until such time as that security might be achieved, they placed far down on their scale of operational priorities the comforts and happiness of the peoples entrusted to their care.

Now the outstanding circumstance concerning the Soviet regime is that down to the present day this process of political consolidation has never been completed and the men in the Kremlin have continued to be predominantly absorbed with the struggle to secure and make absolute the power which they seized in November 1917. They have endeavored to secure it primarily against forces at home, within Soviet society itself. But they have also endeavored to secure it against the outside world. For ideology, as we have seen, taught them that the outside world was hostile and that it was their duty eventually to overthrow the political forces beyond their borders. The powerful hands of Russian history and tradition reached up to sustain them in this feeling. Finally, their own aggressive intransigence with respect to the outside world began to find its own reaction; and they were soon forced, to use another Gibbonesque phrase, "to chastise the contumacy" which they themselves had provoked. It is an undeniable privilege of every man to prove himself right in the thesis that the world is his enemy; for if he reiterates it frequently enough and makes it the background of his conduct he is bound eventually to be right.

Now it lies in the nature of the mental world of the Soviet leaders, as well as in the character of their ideology, that no opposition to them can be officially recognized as having any merit or justification whatsoever. Such opposition can flow, in theory, only from the hostile and incorrigible forces of dying capitalism. As long as remnants of capitalism were officially recognized as existing in Russia, it was possible to place on them, as an internal element, part of the blame for the maintenance of a dictatorial form of society. But as these remnants were liquidated, little by little, this justification fell away; and when it was indicated officially that they had been finally destroyed, it disappeared altogether. And this fact created one of the most basic of the compulsions which came to act upon the Soviet regime: since capitalism no longer existed in Russia and since it could not be admitted that there could be serious or widespread opposition to the Kremlin springing spontaneously from the liberated masses under its authority, it became necessary to justify the retention of the dictatorship by stressing the menace of capitalism abroad.

This began at an early date. In 1924, Stalin specifically defended the retention of the "organs of suppression," meaning, among others, the army and the secret police, on the ground that "as long as there is a capitalist encirclement there will be danger of intervention with all the consequences that flow from that danger." In accordance with that theory, and from that time on, all internal opposition forces in Russia have consistently been portrayed as the agents of foreign forces of reaction antagonistic to Soviet power.

By the same token, tremendous emphasis has been placed on the original Communist thesis of a basic antagonism between the capitalist and Socialist worlds. It is clear, from many indications, that this emphasis is not founded in reality. The real facts concerning it have been confused by the existence abroad of genuine resentment provoked by Soviet philosophy and tactics and occasionally by the existence of great centers of military power, notably the Nazi regime in Germany and the Japanese Government of the late 1930's, which did indeed have aggressive designs against the Soviet Union. But there is ample evidence that the stress laid in Moscow on the menace confronting Soviet society from the world outside its borders is founded not in the realities of foreign antagonism but in the necessity of explaining away the maintenance of dictatorial authority at home.

Now the maintenance of this pattern of Soviet power, namely, the pursuit of unlimited authority domestically, accompanied by the cultivation of the semi-myth of implacable foreign hostility, has gone far to shape the actual machinery of Soviet power as we know it today. Internal organs of administration which did not serve this purpose withered on the vine. Organs which did serve this purpose became vastly swollen. The security of Soviet power came to rest on the iron discipline of the Party, on the severity and ubiquity of the secret police, and on the uncompromising economic monopolism of the state. The "organs of suppression," in which the Soviet leaders had sought security from rival forces, became in large measure the masters of those whom they were designed to serve. Today the major part of the structure of Soviet power is committed to the perfection of the dictatorship and to the maintenance of the concept of Russia as in a state of siege, with the enemy lowering beyond the walls. And the millions of human beings who form that part of the structure of power must defend at all costs this concept of Russia's position, for without it they are themselves superfluous.

As things stand today, the rulers can no longer dream of parting with these organs of suppression. The quest for absolute power, pursued now for nearly three decades with a ruthlessness unparalleled (in scope at least) in modern times, has again produced internally, as it did externally, its own reaction. The excesses of the police apparatus have fanned the potential opposition to the regime into something far greater and more dangerous than it could have been before those excesses began.

But least of all can the rulers dispense with the fiction by which the maintenance of dictatorial power has been defended. For this fiction has been canonized in Soviet philosophy by the excesses already committed in its name; and it is now anchored in the Soviet structure of thought by bonds far greater than those of mere ideology.

II

So much for the historical background. What does it spell in terms of the political personality of Soviet power as we know it today?

Of the original ideology, nothing has been officially junked. Belief is maintained in the basic badness of capitalism, in the inevitability of its destruction, in the obligation of the proletariat to assist in that destruction and to take power into its own hands. But stress has come to be laid primarily on those concepts which relate most specifically to the Soviet regime itself: to its position as the sole truly Socialist regime in a dark and misguided world, and to the relationships of power within it.

The first of these concepts is that of the innate antagonism between capitalism and Socialism. We have seen how deeply that concept has become imbedded in foundations of Soviet power. It has profound implications for Russia's conduct as a member of international society. It means that there can never be on Moscow's side any sincere assumption of a community of aims between the Soviet Union and powers which are regarded as capitalism. It must invariably be assumed in Moscow that the aims of the capitalist world are antagonistic to the Soviet regime and, therefore, to the interests of the peoples it controls. If the Soviet Government occasionally sets its signature to documents which would indicate the contrary, this is to be regarded as a tactical maneuver permissible in dealing with the enemy (who is without honor) and should be taken in the spirit of *caveat emptor*. Basically, the antagonism remains. It is postulated. And from it flow many of the phenomena which we find disturbing in the Kremlin's conduct of foreign policy: the secretiveness, the lack of frankness, the duplicity, the war suspiciousness, and the basic unfriendliness of purpose. These phenomena are there to stay, for the foreseeable future. There can be variations of degree and of emphasis. When there is something the Russians want from us, one or the other of these features of their policy may be thrust temporarily into the background; and when that happens there will always be Americans who will leap forward with gleeful announcements that "the Russians have changed," and some who will even try to take credit for having brought about such "changes." But we should not be misled by tactical maneuvers. These characteristics of Soviet policy, like the postulate from which they flow, are basic to the internal nature of Soviet power, and will be with us, whether in the foreground or the background, until the internal nature of Soviet power is changed.

This means that we are going to continue for a long time to find the Russians difficult to deal with. It does not mean that they should be considered as embarked upon a do-or-die pro-

gram to overthrow our society by a given date. The theory of
the inevitability of the eventual fall of capitalism has the fortunate connotation that there is no hurry about it. The forces
of progress can take their time in preparing the final *coup de
grâce*. Meanwhile, what is vital is that the "Socialist father-
land"—that oasis of power which has been already won for
Socialism in the person of the Soviet Union—should be cher-
ished and defended by all good Communists at home and
abroad, its fortunes promoted, its enemies badgered and con-
founded. The promotion of premature, "adventuristic" revolutionary projects abroad which might embarrass Soviet
power in any way would be an inexcusable, even a counter-
revolutionary act. The cause of Socialism is the support and
promotion of Soviet power, as defined in Moscow.

This brings us to the second of the concepts important to
contemporary Soviet outlook. That is the infallibility of the
Kremlin. The Soviet concept of power, which permits no focal
points of organization outside the Party itself, requires that
the Party leadership remain in theory the sole repository of
truth. For if truth were to be found elsewhere, there would be
justification for its expression in organized activity. But it is
precisely that which the Kremlin cannot and will not permit.

The leadership of the Communist Party is therefore always
right, and has been always right ever since in 1929 Stalin for-
malized his personal power by announcing that decisions of the
Politburo were being taken unanimously.

On the principle of infallibility there rests the iron discipline of the Communist Party. In fact, the two concepts are
mutually self-supporting. Perfect discipline requires recognition of infallibility. Infallibility requires the observance of
discipline. And the two together go far to determine the be-
haviorism of the entire Soviet apparatus of power. But their
effect cannot be understood unless a third factor be taken into
account: namely, the fact that the leadership is at liberty to

put forward for tactical purposes any particular thesis which it finds useful to the cause at any particular moment and to require the faithful and unquestioning acceptance of that thesis by the members of the movement as a whole. This means that truth is not a constant but is actually created, for all intents and purposes, by the Soviet leaders themselves. It may vary from week to week, from month to month. It is nothing absolute and immutable—nothing which flows from objective reality. It is only the most recent manifestation of the wisdom of those in whom the ultimate wisdom is supposed to reside, because they represent the logic of history. The accumulative effect of these factors is to give to the whole subordinate apparatus of Soviet power an unshakeable stubbornness and steadfastness in its orientation. This orientation can be changed at will by the Kremlin but by no other power. Once a given party line has been laid down on a given issue of current policy, the whole Soviet governmental machine, including the mechanism of diplomacy, moves inexorably along the prescribed path, like a persistent toy automobile wound up and headed in a given direction, stopping only when it meets with some unanswerable force. The individuals who are the components of this machine are unamenable to argument or reason which comes to them from outside sources. Their whole training has taught them to mistrust and discount the glib persuasiveness of the outside world. Like the white dog before the phonograph, they hear only the "master's voice." And if they are to be called off from the purposes last dictated to them, it is the master who must call them off. Thus the foreign representative cannot hope that his words will make any impression on them. The most that he can hope is that they will be transmitted to those at the top, who are capable of changing the party line. But even those are not likely to be swayed by any normal logic in the words of the bourgeois representative. Since there can be no appeal to common purposes, there can be no appeal to common mental approaches. For this reason, facts speak louder than words to the ears of the Kremlin; and words carry the greatest weight when they have the ring of reflecting, or being backed up by, facts of unchallengeable validity.

But we have seen that the Kremlin is under no ideological compulsion to accomplish its purposes in a hurry. Like the Church, it is dealing in ideological concepts which are of long-term validity, and it can afford to be patient. It has no right to risk the existing achievements of the revolution for the sake of vain baubles of the future. The very teachings of Lenin himself require great caution and flexibility in the pursuit of Communist purposes. Again, these precepts are fortified by the lessons of Russian history: of centuries of obscure battles between nomadic forces over the stretches of a vast unfortified plain. Here caution, circumspection, flexibility and deception are the valuable qualities; and their value finds natural appreciation in the Russian or the oriental mind. Thus the Kremlin has no compunction about retreating in the face of superior force. And being under the compulsion of no timetable, it does not get panicky under the necessity for such retreat. Its political action is a fluid stream which moves constantly, wherever it is permitted to move, toward a given goal. Its main concern is to make sure that it has filled every nook and cranny available to it in the basin of world power. But if it finds unassailable barriers in its path, it accepts these philosophically and accommodates itself to them. The main thing is that there should always be pressure, increasing constant pressure, toward the desired goal. There is no trace of any feeling in Soviet psychology that that goal must be reached at any given time.

These considerations make Soviet diplomacy at once easier and more difficult to deal with than the diplomacy of individual aggressive leaders like Napoleon and Hitler. On the one hand it is more sensitive to contrary force, more ready to yield on individual sectors of the diplomatic front when that force is felt to be too strong, and thus more rational in the logic and rhetoric of power. On the other hand it cannot be easily defeated or discouraged by a single victory on the part of its opponents. And the patient persistence by which it is animated means that it can be effectively countered not by sporadic acts which represent the momentary whims of democratic opinion but only by intelligent long-range policies on the part of Russia's adversaries—policies no less steady in their purpose, and no less variegated and resourceful in their application, than those of the Soviet Union itself.

In these circumstances it is clear that the main element of any United States policy toward the Soviet Union must be that of a long-term, patient but firm and vigilant containment of Russian expansive tendencies. It is important to note, however, that such a policy has nothing to do with outward histrionics: with threats or blustering or superfluous gestures of outward "toughness." While the Kremlin is basically flexible in its reaction to political realities, it is by no means unamenable to considerations of prestige. Like almost any other government, it can be placed by tactless and threatening gestures in a position where it cannot afford to yield even though this might be dictated by its sense of realism. The Russian leaders are keen judges of human psychology, and as such they are highly conscious that loss of temper and of self-control is never a source of strength in political affairs. They are quick to exploit such evidences of weakness. For these reasons, it is a *sine qua non* of successful dealing with Russia that the foreign government in question should remain at all times cool and collected and that its demands on Russian policy should be put forward in such a manner as to leave the way open for a compliance not too detrimental to Russian prestige.

III

In the light of the above, it will be clearly seen that the Soviet pressure against the free institutions of the Western world is something that can be contained by the adroit and vigilant application of counter-force at a series of constantly shifting geographical and political points, corresponding to the shifts and maneuvers of Soviet policy, but which cannot be charmed or talked out of existence. The Russians look forward to a duel of infinite duration, and they see that already they have scored great successes. It must be borne in mind that there was a time when the Communist Party represented far more of a minority in the sphere of Russian national life than Soviet power today represents in the world community.

But if ideology convinces the rulers of Russia that truth is on their side and that they can therefore afford to wait, those of us on whom that ideology has no claim are free to examine objectively the validity of that premise. The Soviet thesis not only implies complete lack of control by the West over its own economic destiny, it likewise assumes Russian unity, discipline and patience over an infinite period. Let us bring this apocalyptic vision down to earth, and suppose that the Western world finds the strength and resourcefulness to contain Soviet power over a period of ten to fifteen years. What does that spell for Russia itself?

The Soviet leaders, taking advantage of the contributions of modern technique to the arts of despotism, have solved the question of obedience within the confines of their power. Few challenge their authority; and even those who do are unable to make that challenge valid as against the organs of suppression of the state.

The Kremlin has also proved able to accomplish its purpose of building up in Russia, regardless of the interests of the inhabitants, an industrial foundation of heavy metallurgy, which is, to be sure, not yet complete but which is neverthe-less continuing to grow and is approaching those of the other major industrial countries. All of this, however, both the maintenance of internal political security and the building of heavy industry, has been carried out at a terrible cost in hu-man life and in human hopes and energies. It has necessitated the use of forced labor on a scale unprecedented in modern times under conditions of peace. It has involved the neglect or abuse of other phases of Soviet economic life, particularly agriculture, consumers' goods production, housing and trans-portation.

To all that, the war has added its tremendous toll of de-struction, death and human exhaustion. In consequence of this, we have in Russia today a population which is physically and spiritually tired. The mass of the people are disillusioned, skeptical and no longer as accessible as they once were to the magical attraction which Soviet power still radiates to its followers abroad. The avidity with which people seized upon the slight respite accorded to the Church for tactical reasons during the war was eloquent testimony to the fact that their capacity for faith and devotion found little expression in the purposes of the regime.

In these circumstances, there are limits to the physical and nervous strength of people themselves. These limits are abso-lute ones, and are binding even for the cruelest dictatorship, because beyond them people cannot be driven. The forced la-bor camps and the other agencies of constraint provide tem-porary means of compelling people to work longer hours than their own volition or mere economic pressure would dictate; but if people survive them at all they become old before their time and must be considered as human casualties to the de-mands of dictatorship. In either case their best powers are no longer available to society and can no longer be enlisted in the service of the state.

Here only the younger generation can help. The younger generation, despite all vicissitudes and sufferings, is numerous and vigorous; and the Russians are a talented people. But it still remains to be seen what will be the effects on mature performance of the abnormal emotional strains of childhood which Soviet dictatorship created and which were enormously increased by the war. Such things as normal security and placidity of home environment have practically ceased to exist in the Soviet Union outside of the most remote farms and villages. And observers are not yet sure whether that is not going to leave its mark on the over-all capacity of the generation now coming into maturity.

In addition to this, we have the fact that Soviet economic development, while it can list certain formidable achievements, has been precariously spotty and uneven. Russian Communists who speak of the "uneven development of capitalism" should blush at the contemplation of their own national economy. Here certain branches of economic life, such as the metallurgical and machine industries, have been pushed out of all proportion to other sectors of economy. Here is a nation striving to become in a short period one of the great industrial nations of the world while it still has no highway network worthy of the name and only a relatively primitive network of railways. Much has been done to increase efficiency of labor and to teach primitive peasants something about the operation of machines. But maintenance is still a crying deficiency of all Soviet economy. Construction is hasty and poor in quality. Depreciation must be enormous. And in vast sectors of economic life it has not yet been possible to instill into labor anything like that general culture of production and technical self-respect which characterizes the skilled worker of the West.

It is difficult to see how these deficiencies can be corrected at an early date by a tired and dispirited population working largely under the shadow of fear and compulsion. And as long as they are not overcome, Russia will remain economically a vulnerable, and in a certain sense an impotent, nation, capable of exporting its enthusiasms and of radiating the strange charm of its primitive political vitality but unable to back up those articles of export by the real evidences of material power and prosperity.

Meanwhile, a great uncertainty hangs over the political life of the Soviet Union. That is the uncertainty involved in the transfer of power from one individual or group of individuals to others.

This is, of course, outstandingly the problem of the personal position of Stalin. We must remember that his succession to Lenin's pinnacle of preeminence in the Communist movement was the only such transfer of individual authority which the Soviet Union has experienced. That transfer took twelve years to consolidate. It cost the lives of millions of people and shook the state to its foundations, the attendant tremors were felt all through the international revolutionary movement, to the disadvantage of the Kremlin itself.

It is always possible that another transfer of preeminent power may take place quietly and inconspicuously, with no repercussions anywhere. But again, it is possible that the questions involved may unleash, to use some of Lenin's words, one of those "incredibly swift transitions" from "delicate deceit" to "wild violence" which characterize Russian history, and may shake Soviet power to its foundations.

But this is not only a question of Stalin himself. There has been, since 1938, a dangerous congealment of political life in the higher circles of Soviet power. The All-Union Party Congress, in theory the supreme body of the Party, is supposed to meet not less often than once in three years. It will soon be eight full years since its last meeting. During this period membership in the Party has numerically doubled. Party mortality during the war was enormous, and today well over half of the Party members are persons who have entered since the last Party congress was held. Meanwhile, the same small group of men has carried on at the top through an amazing series of national vicissitudes. Surely there is some reason why the experiences of the war brought basic political changes to every one of the great governments of the West. Surely the causes of that phenomenon are basic enough to be present somewhere in the obscurity of Soviet political life, as well. And yet no recognition has been given to these causes in Russia.

It must be surmised from this that even within so highly disciplined an organization as the Communist Party there must be a growing divergence in age, outlook and interest between the great mass of Party members, only so recently recruited into the movement, and the little self-perpetuating clique of men at the top, whom most of these Party members have never met, with whom they have never conversed, and with whom they can have no political intimacy.

Who can say whether, in these circumstances, the eventual rejuvenation of the higher spheres of authority (which can only be a matter of time) can take place smoothly and peacefully, or whether rivals in the quest for higher power will not eventually reach down into these politically immature and inexperienced masses in order to find support for their respective claims. If this were ever to happen, strange consequences could flow for the Communist Party: for the membership at large has been exercised only in the practices of iron discipline and obedience and not in the arts of compromise and accommodation. And if disunity were ever to seize and paralyze the Party, the chaos and weakness of Russian society would be revealed in forms beyond description. For we have seen that Soviet power is only a crust concealing an amorphous mass of human beings among whom no independent organizational structure is tolerated. In Russia there is not even such a thing as local government. The present generation of Russians have never known spontaneity of collective action. If, consequently, anything were ever to occur to disrupt the unity and efficacy of the Party as a political instrument, Soviet Russia might be changed overnight from one of the strongest to one of the weakest and most pitiable of national societies.

Thus the future of Soviet power may not be by any means as secure as Russian capacity for self-delusion would make it appear to the men in the Kremlin. That they can keep power themselves, they have demonstrated. That they can quietly and easily turn it over to others remains to be proved. Meanwhile, the hardships of their rule and the vicissitudes of international life have taken a heavy toll of the strength and hopes of the great people on whom their power rests. It is curious to note that the ideological power of Soviet authority is strongest today in areas beyond the frontiers of Russia, beyond the reach of its police power. This phenomenon brings to mind a comparison used by Thomas Mann in his great novel *Buddenbrooks*. Observing that human institutions often show the greatest outward brilliance at a moment when inner decay is in reality farthest advanced, he compared the Buddenbrook family, in the days of its greatest glamour to one of those stars whose light shines most brightly on this world when in reality it has long since ceased to exist. And who can say with assurance that the strong light still cast by the Kremlin on the dissatisfied peoples of the Western world is not the powerful afterglow of a constellation which is in actuality on the wane? This cannot be proved. And it cannot be disproved. But the possibility remains (and in the opinion of this writer it is a strong one) that Soviet power, like the capitalist world of its conception, bears within it the seeds of its own decay, and that the sprouting of these seeds is well advanced.

IV

It is clear that the United States cannot expect in the foreseeable future to enjoy political intimacy with the Soviet regime. It must continue to regard the Soviet Union as a rival, not a partner, in the political arena. It must continue to expect that Soviet policies will reflect no abstract love of peace and stability, no real faith in the possibility of a permanent happy coexistence of the Socialist and capitalist worlds, but rather a cautious, persistent pressure toward the disruption and weakening of all rival influence and rival power.

Balanced against this are the facts that Russia, as opposed to the Western world in general, is still by far the weaker party, that Soviet policy is highly flexible, and that Soviet society may well contain deficiencies which will eventually weaken its own total potential. This would of itself warrant the United States entering with reasonable confidence upon a policy of firm containment, designed to confront the Russians with unalterable counter-force at every point where they show signs of encroaching upon the interests of a peaceful and stable world.

But in actuality the possibilities for American policy are by no means limited to holding the line and hoping for the best. It is entirely possible for the United States to influence by its actions the internal developments, both within Russia and throughout the international Communist movement, by which Russian policy is largely determined. This is not only a question of the modest measure of informational activity which this government can conduct in the Soviet Union and elsewhere, although that, too, is important. It is rather a question of the degree to which the United States can create among the peoples of the world generally the impression of a country which knows what it wants, which is coping successfully with the problems of its internal life and with the responsibilities of a World Power, and which has a spiritual vitality capable of holding its own among the major ideological currents of the time. To the extent that such an impression can be created and maintained, the aims of Russian Communism must appear sterile and quixotic, the hopes and enthusiasm of Moscow's supporters must wane, and added strain must be imposed on the Kremlin's foreign policies. For the palsied decrepitude of the capitalist world is the keystone of Communist philosophy. Even the failure of the United States to experience the early economic depression which the ravens of the Red Square have been predicting with such complacent confidence since hostilities ceased would have deep and important repercussions throughout the Communist world.

By the same token, exhibitions of indecision, disunity and internal disintegration within this country have an exhilarating effect on the whole Communist movement. At each evidence of these tendencies, a thrill of hope and excitement goes through the Communist world; a new jauntiness can be noted in the Moscow tread; new groups of foreign supporters climb on to what they can only view as the band wagon of international politics; and Russian pressure increases all along the line in international affairs.

It would be an exaggeration to say that American behavior unassisted and alone could exercise a power of life and death over the Communist movement and bring about the early fall of Soviet power in Russia. But the United States has it in its power to increase enormously the strains under which Soviet policy must operate, to force upon the Kremlin a far greater degree of moderation and circumspection than it has had to observe in recent years, and in this way to promote tendencies which must eventually find their outlet in either the break-up or the gradual mellowing of Soviet power. For no mystical, Messianic movement—and particularly not that of the Kremlin—can face frustration indefinitely without eventually adjusting itself in one way or another to the logic of that state of affairs.

Thus the decision will really fall in large measure in this country itself. The issue of Soviet-American relations is in essence a test of the over-all worth of the United States as a nation among nations. To avoid destruction the United States need only measure up to its own best traditions and prove itself worthy of preservation as a great nation.

Surely, there was never a fairer test of national quality than this. In the light of these circumstances, the thoughtful observer of Russian-American relations will find no cause for complaint in the Kremlin's challenge to American society. He will rather experience a certain gratitude to a Providence which, by providing the American people with this implacable challenge, has made their entire security as a nation dependent on their pulling themselves together and accepting the responsibilities of moral and political leadership that history plainly intended them to bear.

AMERICA AND THE RUSSIAN FUTURE*

☼

I

THE very virulence with which Americans reject the outlook and practice of those who now hold power in the Kremlin implies in the strongest possible way the belief in, and desire for, an alternative—for some other Russian outlook and some other set of practices in Russia to take the place of those we know today. Yet we may be permitted to ask whether there is any clear image in our minds of what that outlook and those practices might be, and of the ways by which Americans might promote progress toward them. At the present time, in particular, when the coexistence of the two systems on the same planet has led to such immense strains and anxieties everywhere, and to so much despair of its successful continuation, there is a tendency on the part of many people to permit the image of a different and more acceptable Russia to become eclipsed by, or even identified with, the question of victory or defeat in a future war. Some Americans are already reverting, merely in contemplation of a possible war, to the American bad habit of assuming that there is something final and positive about a military decision—that it is the ending of something, and the happy ending, rather than a beginning.

There could, of course, be no greater error than this, quite apart from any consideration of the blood and sacrifice which war involved. A war against Soviet power which could be said to be relatively successful militarily (and we would do well to remember that no such war could be more than relatively suc-

* Reprinted, by permission of the editor, from *Foreign Affairs*, XXIX, No. 3 (April, 1951), 351–70. Copyright 1951 by Council on Foreign Relations, Inc.

cessful) would in itself assure little or nothing in the way of progress toward the achievement of the sort of alternative we might wish; at the most it would only make more immediate various aspects of a problem which already exists and which every American who objects to Soviet behavior must, in consistency, have in mind anyway, war or no war. That is the problem of the kind of Russia which we would prefer to see; the kind with which we ourselves could, let us say, live easily; the kind which would permit the existence of a much more stable world order; the kind to which it would be both realistic and suitable for us to aspire.

This problem of the possibility of a different and preferable Russia is not really a question of war or peace. War in itself will not bring about such a Russia. Indeed it would be most unlikely to lead in that direction unless accompanied by many wise and strenuous efforts besides the military one. And a continued absence of major war will not preclude the coming of a different Russia. All of that depends upon a great many other things which would have to be done by a great many people, either in war or in peace. Not all of these things can be done by Americans. So far as direct action is concerned, the bulk of them cannot be. But our possibilities for influencing the outcome are significant; and we must remember that there may be times when our efforts may be capable of swinging the balance one way or the other. For that reason our own relationship to the Russian future is something worth our most strenuous thought and attention. And in our efforts to determine it, two things are of major importance: (1) that we should know what we want; and (2) that we should know how to conduct ourselves in order to facilitate, rather than to impede, the coming into being of what we want. The word "facilitate" is used advisedly; for we are dealing here with a foreign country, and our role can be at best a marginal one, supplementary to a far more important role which others must play.

II

What sort of Russia would we like to see before us, as our partner in the world community?

Perhaps the first thing to get straight here is the sort of Russia there is no use looking for. And such a Russia—the kind we may *not* look for—is easy to describe and envisage, for it would be a capitalistic and liberal-democratic one, with institutions closely resembling those of our own republic.

If we look first at the question of the economic system, we see at once that Russia has scarcely known private enterprise as we are familiar with it in this country. Even in pre-Revolutionary times the Russian Government always had a close hold on a number of economic activities, notably transportation and the armament industry, which in our country have traditionally, or at least normally, been private. There were, to be sure, in the earlier period of Russian history, distinguished families of private Russian enterpreneurs, famous for their bold commercial pioneering in the undeveloped areas of the realm. But by and large indigenous private capital remained more conspicuous in the exchange than in the production of commodities. The great domestic business was trade, rather than manufacture. And business did not stand in so high repute as in the West. There was a traditional, and deeply Russian, merchant class; but it was not generally noted or respected for breadth of outlook or for any enlightened concept of its own responsibility to society. The portrayals of it in Russian literature are generally negative and depressing. The members of the landed gentry, whose tastes and prejudices were authoritative in the social field, often looked down on business, and themselves tended to avoid participation in it. The Russian language, in fact, never acquired a word comparable to our expression "businessman"; it had only the word for "merchant," and this term did not always have a pleasant connotation.

As Russia became industrialized, in a sudden rush of activity which took place around the turn of the century, there were clearly apparent the absence of an adequate tradition of responsibility and restraint, on the part of the state and of society generally, to cope with the new strains. This industrial development, proceeding largely on a basis of individual enterprise rather than of widely distributed corporative ownership, was marked by sudden accumulations of fortunes in the hands of individuals and families not always well prepared for such affluence. Often the mode of expenditure of wealth appeared to other people as little creditable as the means by which it had been accumulated. Individual capitalists and workers lived in close proximity—indeed, many of the factory owners lived in the compounds of their factories. Such conditions often bore greater resemblance to the pattern of early Industrial-Revolution capitalism, as Marx had described it, than to conditions in advanced Western countries. This fact may well have had something to do with the success of Marxism in Russia. The Russian industrial capitalist was generally visible in the flesh, and as often as not he had the rotundity, and sometimes (not always) the vulgarity and callousness, of the capitalist of the early-Communist caricature.

All these things go to show that whatever private enterprise may have been in Tsarist Russia, it had not yet come to hold anything resembling the respect and significance in the eyes of the people that it had acquired in the older mercantile countries by the beginning of this century. Perhaps with time it would have. The prospects were steadily improving. Examples of efficient and progressive industrial management existed in Russia before the Revolution, and were increasing.

But all this, it must be remembered, was a long time ago. Thirty-three years have elapsed since the Revolution. Those years, in the strenuous conditions of Soviet life, have witnessed the passing of a full generation. Of the people capable of influencing the course of events in Russia today only an insignificant minority recall the pre-Revolutionary days at all. The younger generation has no comprehension or concept of anything but the state capitalism that the Soviet regime has enforced. And what we are talking about here is something not even in the present but in the indefinite future.

Bearing all this in mind, we see that there is no Russian national understanding which would permit the early establishment in Russia of anything resembling the private enterprise system as we know it. This is not to say that some such understanding will not some day develop. It may, if circumstances are favorable. But it will never be a system identical to our own. And no one will usefully be able to force the pace, particularly no one from outside.

It is true that the term "Socialism" has been used for so many years in close intimacy with the term "Soviet" that it is now hateful to many people, both within and without the borders of the Soviet Union. But it is easy to draw wrong conclusions from this phenomenon. It is conceivable that retail trade and the performance of the small individual services which have so much to do with the pleasantness of daily life may some day return in large measure to private hands in Russia. In agriculture, as we shall see presently, there will certainly be an extensive return to private ownership and initiative. There is a further possibility that the system of mutual production-cooperation by groups of artisans (*artels*)—a system peculiarly rooted in Russian tradition and understanding —may some day point the way to economic institutions which could represent a highly important and promising innovation in the approach to modern problems of labor and capital. But large sections of economic life known to us as the normal provinces of private enterprise will amost certainly remain in na-

tional hands for a long time to come in Russia, regardless of
the identity of the political authority. This should surprise no
American, nor should it offend any. There is no reason why the
form of Russian economic life, beyond certain major exceptions that will be mentioned below, should be considered a
matter of vital concern to the outside world.

Agriculture deserves a special place in our thinking on this
subject. Agricultural enterprise is the Achilles heel of the Soviet system. Left in private hands, it constitutes a concession
to human freedom and individual initiative—a concession
which the true Bolshevik finds abhorrent. Forcibly collec-
tivized, it requires an elaborate apparatus of restraint if the
farmer is to be made to stay on his land and to produce. The
forced collectivization of the farming population is probably today the greatest single cause of discontent in the Soviet
Union, except possibly the excessive cruelty of the police, with
which it is intimately connected. It may be taken for granted
that one of the first acts of any future progressive authority in
Russia would be to abolish this hated system of agricultural
serfdom and to restore to the farmers the pride and incentives
of private land ownership and free disposal of agricultural
commodities. Collective farms may continue to exist; and
they probably will, for the most abhorrent feature of the present system is not the concept of producer-cooperation itself
but the element of restraint that underlies its application. The
collectives of the future will be voluntary cooperatives, however, not shotgun marriages.

Turning to the political side, it was said above that we
could not expect to see the emergence of a liberal-democratic
Russia along American patterns. This cannot be too strongly
emphasized. It does not mean that future Russian regimes will
necessarily be unliberal. There is no liberal tradition finer than
the strain which has existed in the Russia of the past. Many
Russian individuals and groups of this day are deeply imbued

with that tradition, and will do all in their power to make it the dominant element in the Russian future. In that effort, we may wish them well without reservation. But we will be doing them no favor if we permit ourselves to expect too much to happen too fast, or look to them to produce anything resembling our own institutions. These Russian liberals will have no easy road to walk. They will find in their country a young generation that has known nothing but Soviet power and has been trained to think subconsciously in the terms of that power even when it has resented and hated it. Many features of the Soviet system will stick, if only for the reason that everything has been destroyed which might seem to have constituted an alternative to them. And some features will deserve to stick, for no system that lasts over decades is entirely without merits. Any program of government for a future Russia will have to adjust itself to the fact that there has been this Soviet interlude, and that it has left its positive marks as well as its negative ones. And no members of future Russian governments will be aided by doctrinaire and impatient well-wishers in the West who look to them, just because they are seeking a decent alternative to what we know today as Bolshevism, to produce in short order a replica of the Western democratic dream.

Above all, it behooves us Americans, in this connection, to repress, and if possible to extinguish once and for all, our inveterate tendency to judge others by the extent to which they contrive to be like ourselves. In our relations with the people of Russia it is important, as it has never been important before, for us to recognize that our institutions may not have relevance for people living in other climes and conditions and that there can be social structures and forms of government in no way resembling our own and yet not deserving of censure. There is no reason why this realization should shock us. In 1831 de Tocqueville, writing from the United States, correctly observed: "The more I see of this country the more I admit myself penetrated with this truth: that there is nothing absolute in the theoretical value of political institutions, and that their efficiency depends almost always on the original circumstances and the social conditions of the people to whom they are applied."

Forms of government are forged mainly in the fire of practice, not in the vacuum of theory. They respond to national character and to national realities. There is great good in the Russian national character, and the realities of that country scream out today for a form of administration more considerate of that good. Let us hope that it will come. But when Soviet power has run its course, or when its personalities and spirit begin to change (for the ultimate outcome could be of one or the other), let us not hover nervously over the people who come after, applying litmus papers daily to their political complexions to find out whether they answer to our concept of "democratic." Give them time; let them be Russians; let them work out their internal problems in their own manner. The ways by which peoples advance toward dignity and enlightenment in government are things that constitute the deepest and most intimate processes of national life. There is nothing less understandable to foreigners, nothing in which foreign interference can do less good. There are, as we shall see presently, certain features of the future Russian state that *are* of genuine concern to the outside world. But these do not include the form of government itself, provided only that it keep within certain well-defined limits, beyond which lies totalitarianism.

III

What, then, do they include? To what kind of a Russia may we reasonably and justly look forward? What attributes are we, as responsible members of the world community, entitled to look for in the personality of a foreign state, and of Russia in particular?

We may look, in the first place, for a Russian government which, in contrast to the one we know today, would be tolerant, communicative and forthright in its relations with other states and peoples. It would not take the ideological position that its own purposes cannot finally prosper unless all systems of government not under its control are subverted and eventually destroyed. It would dispense with this paranoiac suspiciousness we know so well, and consent to view the outside world, outselves included, as it really is and always has been: neither entirely good nor entirely bad, neither entirely to be trusted nor entirely to be mistrusted (if only for the simple reason that "trust" has only a relative significance in foreign affairs). It would consent to recognize that this outside world is not really preoccupied with diabolical plots to invade Russia and inflict injuries on the Russian people. Viewing the outside world in this way, the statesmen of a future Russia could approach it with tolerance and forbearance and practical good humor, defending their national interests as statesmen must, but not assuming that these can be furthered only at the expense of the interests of others, and vice versa.

No one asks for a naïve and childlike confidence; no one asks for a fatuous enthusiasm for all that is foreign; no one asks that the genuine and legitimate differences of interest which have always marked, and will always continue to mark, the relations between peoples be ignored. We must expect Russian national interests not only to continue to exist but to be vigorously and confidently asserted. But in a regime that we could recognize as an improvement over what we know today we would expect that this would be done in an atmosphere of emotional sanity and moderation: that the foreign representative would not continue to be viewed and treated as one possessed of the devil; that it would be conceded that there might be such a thing as innocent and legitimate curiosity about a foreign country, which could be permitted to be gratified without fatal detriment to that country's national life; that it would be recognized that there might be individual foreign business aspirations which did not aim at the destruction of the Russian state; that it would be admitted, finally, that persons desirous of travelling across international borders might have, and are even apt to have, motives other than ''espionage, sabotage and diversion''—such trivial motives, in fact, as the enjoyment of travel or the peculiar impulses that move people to wish to visit relatives from time to time. In short, we may ask that the grotesque system of anachronisms known as the Iron Curtain be lifted from the world, and that the Russian people, who have so much to give and so much to receive as mature members of the world community, cease to be insulted by a policy that treats them as children, too immature to have normal contact with the adult world, too undependable to be let out alone.

Secondly, while recognizing that the internal system of government is in all essential respects Russia's own business and may well depart drastically from our own, we are entitled to expect that the exercise of governmental authority will stop short of that fairly plain line beyond which lies totalitarianism. Specifically, we may expect that any regime which claims to contrast favorably with that which we have before us today will refrain from enslaving its own labor—industrial and agricultural. There is a reason for this: a reason even more solid than the shock we experience at witnessing the sickening details of this type of oppression. When a regime sets out to enslave its own working population in this way, it requires for the maintenance of the arrangement so vast an apparatus of coercion that the imposition of the Iron Curtain follows almost automatically. No ruling group likes to admit that it can govern its people only by regarding and treating them as criminals. For this reason there is always a tendency to justify internal oppression by pointing to the menacing iniquity of the outside world. And the outside world must be portrayed, in these circumstances, as very iniquitous indeed—iniquitous to the point of caricature. Nothing short of this will do. Carefully hiding the realities behind the Iron Curtain, the regime depicts "abroad" to its own people in every lurid hue of hideousness, as anxious mothers attempt to intimidate their children and fortify their own authority by embroidering the image of that sinister "something" which "will get you if you don't watch out."

In this way, excess of internal authority leads inevitably to unsocial and aggressive conduct as a government among governments, and is a matter of concern to the international community. The world is not only heartily sick of this comedy by reason of the endless and wearisome falsehoods it involves, but it has learned to recognize it as something so irresponsible and dangerous that, maintained for any length of time, it easily becomes a major hazard for world peace and stability. It is for this reason that we, while recognizing that all distinctions as between freedom and authority are relative and admitting that 90 per cent of them are no business of ours when they affect a foreign country, still insist that there is an area here in which no government of a great country can move without creating the most grievous and weighty problems for its neighbors. That is precisely the area in which the regime of Hitler found itself at home, and in which the Soviet Government has moved for at least these past fifteen years. We may state bluntly that we can recognize no future Russian regime as one with which we could have a satisfactory relationship unless it keeps out of this danger area.

The third thing we may hope from a new Russia is that it will refrain from pinning an oppressive yoke on other peoples who have the instinct and the capacity for national self-assertion. In mentioning this matter, we are entering upon a delicate subject. There is no more difficult and treacherous one in the entire lexicon of political issues. In the relationships between the Great-Russian people and nearby peoples outside the confines of the old Tsarist Empire, as well as non-Russian national groups that were included within that empire, there is no conceivable pattern of borders or institutional arrangements which, measured against the concepts prevailing to date, would not arouse violent resentments and involve genuine injustices in many quarters. If people in that part of the world are going to go on thinking of national borders and minority problems in the way that they have thought of them in the past and continue to think of them today, Americans would do well to avoid incurring any responsibility for views or positions on these subjects; for any specific solutions they may advocate will some day become a source of great bitterness against them, and they will find themselves drawn into controversies that have little or nothing to do with the issue of human freedom.

What is plainly necessary, and the only solution worthy of American encouragement, is the rise of such a spirit among all the peoples concerned as would give to border and institutional arrangements in that troubled area an entirely new, and greatly reduced, significance. Whether that spirit will actually arise, we cannot tell. And precisely because we cannot tell this, Americans should be extremely careful in committing their support or encouragement to any specific arrangements in this sphere; for we cannot know what they mean until there is clarity as to the spirit which will underlie them. How can we know whether a given national group will require an independent status, or a federal status, some special brand of local self-government, or no special status at all, until we know something about the psychological climate in which these arrangements would operate? There are peoples of non-Russian ethnological character on the borders of the Great-Russian family whose economic existence is intimately bound up with that of the Great-Russians. The future should see a minimum of disruption of these economic ties, and that in itself would normally warrant a close political connection. But its nature would always have to depend on what sort of attitudes prevailed on both sides of the line: on the degree of tolerance and insight which the peoples involved (and not only the Russian people) might be able to bring to the establishment of these relationships.

We are all agreed, for example, that the Baltic countries should never again be forced against the innermost feelings of their peoples into any relationship whatsoever with a Russian state; but they would themselves be foolish to reject close and cooperative arrangements with a tolerant, nonimperialistic Russia, which genuinely wished to overcome the unhappy memories of the past and to place her relations to the Baltic peoples on a basis of real respect and disinterestedness. The Ukraine, again, deserves full recognition for the peculiar genius and abilities of its people and for the requirements and possibilities of its development as a linguistic and cultural entity; but the Ukraine is economically as much a part of Russia as Pennsylvania is a part of the United States. Who can say what the final status of the Ukraine should be unless he knows the character of the Russia to which the adjustment will have to be made? As for the satellite states: they must, and will, recover their full independence; but they will not assure themselves of a stable and promising future if they make the mistake of proceeding from feelings of revenge and hatred toward the Russian people who have shared their tragedy, and if they try to base that future on the exploitation of the initial difficulties of a well-intentioned Russian regime struggling to overcome the legacy of Bolshevism.

There is no use underestimating the bitterness of these territorial problems, even assuming the utmost of goodwill and relaxed tolerance on the part of the peoples concerned. Some of the dispositions taken at the close of the Second World War (made even worse today by the deliberate policy on the part of certain governments to turn the provisional prematurely into the permanent) represent distinctly unhealthy situations, not conducive to a peaceful future. Some day these dispositions must be changed; and it will admittedly require tact on the part of all concerned, and forbearance bordering on the miraculous, if these changes are to be effected without a further compounding of violence and bitterness. For that unhappy situation the peoples of Europe have to thank the calculating cynicism of the Bolshevik leaders and the amiable indulgence of the Western Powers.

But one of the greatest of the German oppositionists in the time of Hitler, writing at the risk of his life to a friend in England during the recent war, said: "For us Europe after the war is less a problem of frontiers and soldiers, of top-heavy organizations and grand plans than . . . a question of how the picture of man can be restored in the breasts of our fellow-citizens."[1]

Would that the Nazi gallows had spared this man for the present and the future; he was both right and courageous, and such people will be desperately needed if the future of the region from the Elbe to Bering Strait is ever to be happier than it has been in the past. An American who wishes his influence to be beneficial in that part of the world would do well to impress on any friends he may have from the Iron Curtain countries the folly of a continuation, by them or anyone else, of these dreary and profitless manipulations with so-called national boundaries and with the naïve loyalties of bewildered linguistic groups which have passed for statesmanship in that

1. *A German of the Resistance: The Last Letters of Count Helmuth James von Moltke* (London: Oxford University Press, 1948).

area in the past. There are more important things than where the border runs, and the first of these is that on both sides of it there should be tolerance and maturity, humility in the face of sufferings of the past and the problems of the future, and a realization that none of the important problems of the future for any of the peoples of Europe is going to be solved entirely, or even primarily, within the country's national boundaries.

These, then, are the things for which an American well-wisher may hope from the Russia of the future: that she lift forever the Iron Curtain, that she recognize certain limitations to the internal authority of government, and that she abandon, as ruinous and unworthy, the ancient game of imperialist expansion and oppression. If she is not prepared to do these things, she will hardly be distinguishable from what we have before us today, and to hasten the arrival of such a Russia would not be worth the care or thought of a single American. If she is prepared to do these things, then Americans will not need to concern themselves more deeply with her nature and purposes; the basic demands of a more stable world order will then have been met, and the area in which a foreign people can usefully have thoughts and suggestions will have been filled.

IV

So much, then, for the kind of Russia we would like to see. How should we, as Americans, conduct ourselves in order to promote the realization of, or at least an advance toward, such a Russia?

In our thinking on this subject we must be careful to distinguish between direct action, i.e., action on our part directly affecting persons and events behind what is now the Iron Curtain, and indirect action, by which we mean action taken with respect to other things—with respect, let us say, to ourselves or to our relations with other people—and affecting the Soviet world only obliquely and incidentally.

Most regrettably, as the world is today, the possibility for direct action by Americans toward the ends discussed above must be examined both in terms of a possible war and in terms of the continuation of the present state of "no major war." The first of these contingencies must unfortunately be discussed first, for it has become the dominant prospect in the minds of many people.

If war comes, what can we do directly to promote the emergence of a more desirable Russia? We can hold steadily and clearly in mind the image of the kind of Russia we would like to see and assure that military operations are shaped in such a way as to permit it to come into existence.

The first part of this task is a negative one: not to let ourselves be diverted by irrelevant or confusing concepts of war aims. We can avoid, this time, the tyranny of slogans. We can avoid confusing ourselves with grandiose and unrealistic, or even meaningless, phrases designed simply to make us feel better about the bloody and terrible business in which we are engaged. We can remember that war—a matter of destruction, brutalization and sacrifice, of separations, domestic disintegration, and the weakening of the deeper fabrics of society— is a process which of itself can achieve no positive aims: that even military victory is only the prerequisite for some further and more positive achievement which it makes possible but by no means assures. We can have the moral courage, this time, to remind ourselves that major international violence is, in terms of the values of our civilization, a form of bankruptcy for us all—even for those who are confident that they are right; that all of us, victors and vanquished alike, must emerge from it poorer than we began it and farther from the goals we had in mind; and that, since victory or defeat can signify only relative degrees of misfortune, even the most glorious military victory would give us no right to face the future in any spirit other than one of sorrow and humbleness for what has happened and of realization that the road ahead, toward a better world, is long and hard—longer and harder, in fact, than it would have been had it been possible to avoid a military cataclysm altogether.

Remembering these things, we will be less inclined to view military operations as ends in themselves, and should find it easier to conduct them in a manner harmonious with our political purposes. If it should fall to us to take up arms against those who today dispose over the Russian people, we can try not to give that people the impression that we are their enemies, or consider them ours. We can try to make them understand the necessity of such hardships as we cannot avoid inflicting on them. We can endeavor to hold constantly before them the evidences of a sympathetic understanding for their past and interest in their future. We can give them the feeling that we are on their side, and that our victory, if it comes, will be used to provide them with a chance to shape their own destiny in the future to a pattern happier than that which they have known in the past. For all of this it is important that we bear in mind what Russia has been, and can be, and not permit political differences to becloud that picture.

National greatness is a difficult thing to define. Every nation is made up of individuals; and among individuals, as is known, there is no uniformity. Some are charming, others irritating; some are honest, others not exactly so; some are strong, others weak; some command admiration, others, by general agreement, are anything but admirable. This is true in our own country; it is true in Russia. Just what, in these circumstances, national greatness consists of, is hard to say. Certainly it rarely consists of those qualities in which a people thinks itself great; for in nations, as in individuals, the outstanding virtues are generally not the ones for which we fancy ourselves distinguished.

Yet that there *is* such a thing as national greatness is clear;

and that the Russian people possess it in high degree is beyond question. They are a people whose progress out of darkness and squalor has been a painful one, marked by enormous sufferings and punctuated by heart-rending setbacks. Nowhere on the face of the globe has the tiny flame of faith in the dignity and charity of man flickered more precariously under the winds that tore at it. Yet it has never gone out; it is not extinguished today even in the heart of the Russian land and whoever studies the struggle of the Russian spirit through the ages can only bare his head in admiration, before those Russian people who kept it alight through their sacrifices and sufferings.

The record of Russian culture to date has proven that this struggle has a significance far wider than the confines of the traditional Russian territory; it is a part, and an extremely important part, of the general cultural progress of mankind. We have only to look at the people of Russian birth or origin living and working in our midst—the engineers, the scientists, the writers, the artists—to know that this is true. It would be tragic if our indignation over Soviet outlooks and policies led us to make ourselves the accomplices of Russian despotism by forgetting the greatness of the Russian people, losing our confidence in their genius and their potential for good, and placing ourselves in opposition to their national feelings. The vital importance of this becomes even clearer when we reflect that we in the outside world who believe in the cause of freedom will never prevail in any struggle against the destructive workings of Soviet power unless the Russian people are our willing allies. That goes for peace, and it goes for war. The Germans, though not fighting at that time in the cause of freedom, learned to their sorrow the impossibility of combatting simultaneously both the Russian people and the Soviet Government.

The greatest difficulty here, of course, lies in the mute and helpless position in which the Russian people find themselves as subjects of a totalitarian regime. Our experiences with Germany have demonstrated that we have not succeeded very well, as a nation, in understanding the position of the man who lives under the yoke of modern despotism. Totalitarianism is not a national phenomenon; it is a disease to which all humanity is in some degree vulnerable. To live under such a regime is a misfortune that can befall a nation by virtue of reasons purely historic and not really traceable to any particular guilt on the part of the nation as a whole. Where circumstances weaken the powers of resistance, to a certain crucial degree, the virus triumphs. If individual life is to go on at all within the totalitarian framework it must go on by arrangement with the regime, and to some extent in connivance with its purposes. Furthermore, there will always be areas in which the totalitarian government will succeed in identifying itself with popular feelings and aspirations. The relationship between citizen and political authority under totalitarianism is therefore inevitably complicated: it is never pat and simple. Who does not understand these things cannot understand what is at stake in our relations with the peoples of such countries. These realities leave no room for our favored conviction that the people of a totalitarian state can be neatly divided into collaborators and martyrs and that there will be none left over. People do not emerge from this relationship unscathed: when they do emerge they need help, guidance and understanding, not scoldings and sermons.

We will get nowhere with an attitude of emotional indignation directed toward an entire people. Let us rise above these easy and childish reactions and consent to view the tragedy of Russia as partly our own tragedy, and the people of Russia as our comrades in the long hard battle for a happier system of man's coexistence with himself and with nature on this troubled planet.

V

So much for what we do if, contrary to our hopes and our wishes, a war so much talked about should prove impossible to avoid. But supposing we are faced with a continuation of the present state of absence of major warfare? What should our course of action be then?

First of all, have we any grounds to hope, in these circumstances, that there might be changes in Russia of the kind that we are here envisaging? There are no objective criteria for the answer to this question. There is no "proof" one way or another. The answer rests on something which is partly a matter of opinion and judgment, but partly, admittedly, an act of faith. The writer believes the answer to be a positive one: that we are indeed justified in hoping, and holding it possible, that there may be such changes. But in substantiation of this view it is possible to say only the following.

There can be no genuine stability in any system which is based on the evil and weakness in man's nature—which attempts to live by man's degradation, feeding like a vulture on his anxieties, his capacity for hatred, his susceptibility to error, and his vulnerability to psychological manipulation. Such a system can represent no more than the particular frustrations and bitterness of the generation of men who created it, and the cold terror of those who have been weak or unwise enough to become its agents.

I am not speaking here of the Russian Revolution as such. That was a more complicated phenomenon, with deeper roots in the logic of history. I am speaking of the process by which something claiming to be a hopeful turn in human events, claiming to lead toward a decrease rather than an increase in the sum total of human injustice and oppression, evolved into the shabby purgatory of the police state. Only men with a profound sense of personal failure could find satisfaction in doing to others those things which are always involved in such a system; and whoever has had occasion to look deeply into the eyes of a Communist police officer will have found there, in that dark well of disciplined hatred and suspicion, the tiny gleam of despairing fright which is the proof of this statement. Those who begin by clothing a personal lust for power and revenge with the staggering deceits and oversimplifications of totalitarianism end up by fighting themselves—in a dreary, hopeless encounter which projects itself onto the subject peoples and makes of their happiness and their faith its battlefield.

Men of this sort can bequeath something of the passion of the struggle to those of their close associates who inherit their power. But the process of inheritance cannot be carried much further. People can move along, themselves, as by some force of habit, on the strength of an emotional drive acquired at second hand; but it is no longer theirs to transmit to others. The impulses that thrust men of one generation into so despairing an attitude toward themselves and toward the popular masses in whom they like to see themselves reflected become progressively uninteresting to succeeding generations. The cruelties, the untruths, the endless deriding of man's nature practised in the concentration camps: all these institutions of the police state, though they may first have something of the lurid fascination that manifestations of danger and anarchy always exert in a well-regulated and composed society, sooner or later end up—like some stale and repetitious pornography—by boring everybody, including those who practise them.

Many of the servants of totalitarian power, it is true, having debased themselves more than their victims and knowing that they have barred themselves from any better future, may cling despairingly to their unhappy offices. But despotism can never live just by the fears of the jailers and hangmen alone; it must have behind it a driving political will. In the days when despotic power could be closely associated with a dynasty or an inherited oligarchy, such a political will could be more enduring. But then, by the same token, it had to take a more benevolent and constructive interest in the people over whom it ruled and from whose labors it fed. It could not afford to live by their total intimidation and degradation. Dynastic continuity compelled it to recognize an obligation to the future, as well as to the present and the past.

The modern police state does not have these qualities. It represents only a fearful convulsion of society, springing from the stimulus of a given historical moment. Society may be grievously, agonizingly ill from it. But society—being something organic, marked by change and renewal and adjustment—will not remain this way indefinitely. The violent maladjustments which caused the convulsion will eventually begin to lose their actuality, and the instinct for a healthier, less morbid, more interesting life will begin to assert itself.

These, then, are the reflections which give the writer, for one, faith that if the necessary alternatives are kept before the Russian people, in the form of the existence elsewhere on this planet of a civilization which is decent, hopeful and purposeful, the day must come—soon or late, and whether by gradual process or otherwise—when that terrible system of power which has set a great people's progress back for decades and has lain like a shadow over the aspirations of all civilization will be distinguishable no longer as a living reality, but only as something surviving partly in recorded history and partly in the sediment of constructive, organic change which every great human upheaval, however unhappy its other manifestations, manages to deposit on the shelf of time.

But how those changes are to come about is something which cannot be foreseen. If there are, indeed, such things as laws of political development, they will surely play a part here; but then they would be the laws of development peculiar to the phenomenon of modern totalitarianism, and these have not yet been adequately studied and understood. Whether such laws exist or not, developments will be modified both by national character and by the tremendous part which the fortuitous unquestionably plays in the shaping of human events.

These things being so, we must admit with respect to the future of government in Russia, we see "as through a glass, darkly." Superficial evidences would not seem to leave much room for hope that the changes we would wish to see in the attitudes and practices of government in Moscow could come about without violent breaks in the continuity of power, that is, without the overthrow of the system. But we cannot be sure of this. Stranger things have happened—though not much stranger. And, in any case, it is not our business to prejudge the question. It is not necessary for us, merely in order to shape our own conduct in a way conducive to our own interests, to decide what we admittedly cannot really know. We should allow, here, for all possibilities, and should exclude none. The main thing is that we keep clearly in mind the image of what we would like to see in the personality of Russia as an actor on the world stage, and let that be our guide in all our dealings with Russian political factions, including both that which is in power and those which are in opposition to it. And if it should turn out to be the will of fate that freedom should come to Russia by erosion from despotism rather than by the violent upthrust of liberty, let us be able to say that our policy was such as to favor it, and that we did not hamper it by preconception or impatience or despair.

Of one thing we may be sure: no great and enduring change in the spirit and practice of government in Russia will ever come about primarily through foreign inspiration or advice. To be genuine, to be enduring and to be worth the hopeful welcome of other peoples such a change would have to flow from the initiatives and efforts of the Russians themselves. It is a shallow view of the workings of history which looks to such things as foreign propaganda and agitation to bring about fundamental changes in the lives of a great nation. Those who talk of overthrowing the Soviet system by propaganda point, by way of justification of their thesis, to the intensive workings of the Soviet propaganda machine and to the various facets of subversive activity conducted, inspired or encouraged by the Kremlin throughout the world. They forget that the outstanding fact about such activities, on the record of the thirty-three years over which they have been assiduously conducted, has been their general failure. In the end, military intimidation or invasion has been generally necessary for the actual spread of the Soviet system. It may be argued that China is an exception to this statement; but to what extent China can really be said to be part of the Soviet system we do not know, and to attribute the revolution which has taken place in China in these recent years primarily to Soviet propaganda or instigation is to underestimate grievously, to say the least, a number of other highly important factors.

Any attempt at direct talking by one nation to another about the latter's political affairs is a questionable procedure, replete with possibilities for misunderstanding and resentment. That is particularly true where spirit and tradition differ and the political terminology is not really translatable. This appreciation in no way weakens the importance of the "Voice of America," the function of which, with respect to Russia, is to reflect as faithfully as possible the atmosphere and attitudes of this country, in order that the Soviet citizen may form a fair judgment of them. But this is an entirely different thing from urgings toward this or that political action. We may have our own hopes or ideas as to the implications for the Soviet citizen of the view of American realities which is apparent in the broadcasts of the "Voice" and in such other evidences of American life as reach his consciousness; we may think we know what we would do in the light of this evidence; but it would be a mistake for us to be too explicit and to make these things the basis of suggestions and promptings to him about what he should do in the internal political life of his own country. We are too apt to talk in our terms rather than his, and from an imperfect understanding of his problems and possibilities. And our words, accordingly, are apt to convey meanings entirely different from those which we meant them to convey.

For these reasons, the most important influence that the United States can bring to bear upon internal developments in Russia will continue to be the influence of example: the influence of what it is, and not only what it is to others but what it is to itself. This is not to say that many of those things which are now preoccupying the public mind are not of unquestioned importance: such things as physical strength, armaments, determination and solidarity with other free nations. It is not to deny the urgent and overriding necessity for a wise and adroit foreign policy, designed to release and make effective all those forces in the world which, together with our own, can serve to convince the masters of the Kremlin that their grand design is a futile and unachievable one, persistence in which promises no solution of their own predicaments and dilemmas. In fact, there can be no question but that these must remain major preoccupations if war is to be avoided and time is to be gained for the working of more hopeful forces. But they can only remain sterile and negative if they are not given meaning and substance by something which goes deeper and looks further ahead than the mere prevention of war or the frustration of imperialistic expansion. To this, there is general agreement; but what is this "something"? Many people think it only a question of what we urge upon others, in other words, a question of external propaganda. I would submit that it is primarily a question of what we urge upon ourselves. It is a question of the spirit and purpose of American national life itself. Any message we may try to bring to others will be effective only if it is in accord with what we are to ourselves, and if this is something sufficiently impressive to compel the respect and confidence of a world which, despite all its material difficulties, is still more ready to recognize and respect spiritual distinction than material opulence.

Our first and main concern must still be to achieve this state of national character. We need worry less about convincing others that we have done so. In the lives of nations the really worthwhile things cannot and will not be hidden. Thoreau wrote: "There is no ill which may not be dissipated, like the dark, if you let in a stronger light upon it. . . . If the light we use is but a paltry and narrow taper, most objects will cast a shadow wider than themselves." Conversely, if our taper is a strong one we may be sure that its rays will penetrate to the Russian room and eventually play their part in dissipating the gloom which prevails there. No iron curtain could suppress, even in the innermost depths of Siberia, the news that America had shed the shackles of disunity, confusion and doubt, had taken a new lease of hope and determination, and was setting about her tasks with enthusiasm and clarity of purpose.

PART III

I

REFLECTIONS ON THE WALGREEN LECTURES

✿

THIRTY-THREE years ago this spring, I went to the University of Chicago to deliver a set of six lectures—this in response to an invitation that I had rather light-heartedly accepted over a year before. I was then still a government official—a foreign service officer, to be exact—but on an extended leave of absence which I was spending at the Institute for Advanced Study in Princeton. These were the first academic lectures I had ever been asked to give. They were addressed to a few episodes from the history of America's external relations. Since I was at that time even more ignorant than I am today of the general history of American diplomacy, I drew primarily on my own twenty-four years of diplomatic experience, and tried to look at the episodes in question from the standpoint of the lessons which that experience had taught.

Well—the lectures were duly published by the University of Chicago Press, in a small volume entitled *American Diplomacy* which appears to have been widely used around the country as outside reading for courses in American diplomatic history and international relations generally, and which, I understand, to my own astonishment, is still in print. Some of you have probably had to read them somewhere along the line—whether to your pleasure or your pain is a question I shall not go into.

Those of you who *have* seen them, in any case, will recall that they were both analytical and critical in character. They were analytical in the sense that I endeavored to discover what was in the minds of the respective American statesmen when they led us into these various excursions into world affairs. And they were critical in the sense that having examined this intellectual and political motivation, I tried to measure it against the realities of the situations to which we conceived ourselves to be reacting, as well as against the results we achieved, and thus to assess the adequacy of the response.

The results of this inquiry were not very encouraging, I am afraid, in the light they threw on the ability of this country to engage itself usefully in ventures far beyond its own frontiers.

The first lecture dealt with the Spanish-American War of 1898, and I found that, in the reasons we had for entering into that war, there was "not much of solemn and careful deliberation" and "not much of prudent and orderly measuring of our national interest." As for the manner in which we employed our armed forces once we had launched ourselves into that war, I found that we were guided not by any very thoughtful concept of what it was we wanted to achieve, and why, but rather by "popular moods, political pressures, and inner-governmental intrigue."

So far as the Open Door episode was concerned, as treated in the second of the lectures, I came to the conclusion that this was a case where American public opinion had been easily bamboozled into viewing as a great act of American statesmanship a diplomatic initiative which was actually no more than a pretentious and useless gesture, addressed to a situation we understood very poorly.

In the third lecture I talked about our relations, respectively with China and Japan over the half century from 1900 to 1950. My conclusion was that these relations had reflected a curious but deeply-rooted sentimentality on our part towards China, arising evidently from the pleasure it gave us to view ourselves as high-minded patrons, benefactors, and teachers of a people seen as less fortunate, and less advanced, than ourselves. And I could not help seeing in this self-indulgence a form of national narcissism—of collective self-admiration —to which it seemed to me, many Americans were prone. This tendency, I thought, could only conceal deep subconscious feelings of insecurity—a need for reassurance about ourselves—something that contrasted very sharply with our pretentious external behavior.

I then turned, in that same lecture, to our negative and critical attitudes towards Japan, which were of course the mirror image of the patronizing and protective attitudes we adopted towards China. Our grievances against Japan seemed to be centered largely on the positions Japan then occupied on the mainland of northeastern Asia—predominantly in Korea and Manchuria. We saw these positions as legally and morally wrong, because in the formal sense these were not

Japanese territories the Japanese were occupying. I took issue with this view, charging that we were trying to apply our own legalistic and moralistic standards to a situation to which they were in reality very little relevant, and argued that instead of setting ourselves up as judges over the morality of others, we would have done better to search for a stable balance of power among the various nationalistic forces active in that region—the Russians, the Chinese, and the Japanese—among whom there was really very little to choose from the standpoint of moral quality. In trying to dig the Japanese out of the positions they occupied on the Asian mainland, we were ignoring, I thought, the strong possibility that if we succeeded in doing this, what filled the resulting vacuums might well be some form of power even less to our liking than the Japanese we had removed. This proved actually to be the case.

It is worth recalling, in that connection, that the lectures I am talking about were delivered during the Korean war; and I could not help but see, in the unhappy position in which we then found ourselves on the Korean peninsula, a form of ironic punishment for our earlier lack of understanding for Japanese interests and for our insistence on removing the Japanese from their position there when we had no hopeful alternatives to suggest. I tried to point out, on the strength of this example, that our choices in foreign policy were not always between good and evil, but more often between the greater and the lesser of two evils.

The fourth lecture was addressed to our involvement in the First World War. The ostensible reason for our entrance into that war in 1917 was, as you may recall, the violation of our neutrality by the Germans; and I pointed out the absurdity of going to war to protect your neutrality—of abandoning your neutrality, that is, for the purpose of protecting it. And then, too, I could not refrain from pointing out the inconsistency of remaining outside a given international conflict as long as we could contrive to do so (as we did in the case of this First World War) but then—when we had been forced into it—suddenly discovering that we were fighting in a great moral cause in which all the values of our civilization were at stake. If the war against imperial Germany really was such a cause (and actually, it was not), then I thought we should not have had to be kicked into participation in the struggle: we should have entered it voluntarily. But if the war was not such a cause, then we should not have allowed ourselves to be provoked into it over so trivial an issue as our neutrality.

As for the Second World War, which was the last of the specific American involvements treated in those lectures, I criticized, once again, the American tendency to idealize, once we were in it, a conflict from which we had remained aloof as long as we could, and which we were only forced into by the Japanese attack on Pearl Harbor and the subsequent declaration of war against us by Germany. But I also stressed our failure, in fact, our refusal, to recognize that any victory we might have in that conflict was actually mortgaged from the outset by the fact that owing to our military weakness and that of our allies, we could hope to defeat Hitler only with the extensive help of the Russians, and that for this indispensable help there was bound to be, as indeed there has been, a heavy price to pay. The present divided and unstable situation of Germany and Europe, reflecting as it does our inability to get to Central Europe faster than the Russians did in 1945, is simply a part of that price. Had we recognized this bitter limitation on the possible results of our armed effort—had we recognized that we were not strong enough to bring this war to the sort of conclusion we would like it to have had—we would, I thought, not have deceived ourselves by rosy dreams of the peaceful and glorious international order to be assured by our victory.

So much for the episodes treated in the Chicago lectures. Let me now mention some of our main involvements in the Far East in the postwar period. And let me begin with Korea.

Remember the situation at the end of the war in the Pacific. We had firmly, and I think rightly, refused to permit the Russians to have any part in the occupation of the defeated Japan. But on the Korean peninsula we ended up, as we did in the center of Europe, with the Soviet forces taking the Japanese surrender in the northern part of the peninsula, and we taking it in the south, but with no agreement as between the two powers about the future of that country.

Now General MacArthur, who was initially the most influential person in determining American policy towards the defeated Japan, seems originally to have envisaged a permanently disarmed and neutralized Japan. It was my own thought (and I still think there was good reason for it) that we should have stuck to that principle. I thought it possible that in return for our consent to a neutralized and demilitarized Japan, which would have meant that that country would not be used as a base for American military or naval forces in the postwar era, the Russians, for whom such a settlement held important advantages, might have been willing to consent to the establishment of a democratically-elected and presumably moderate government in all of Korea.

But by the end of the year 1949 something had happened in Washington that was to have a profound effect on all our postwar policies. The concept of "containment," which I had been so bold as to put forward in 1947, had been addressed to what I and others had believed was a danger of the political expansion of Stalinist communism—and especially the danger that local communists, inspired and controlled by Moscow, might acquire dominant positions in the great defeated industrial countries of Germany and Japan. I did not believe, nor did others who knew the Soviet Union well, that there was the slightest danger of a Soviet military attack against the major western powers or Japan. This was, in other words, a political danger, not a military one. And the historical record bears out that conclusion. But for reasons I have never fully understood, by 1949 a great many people in Washington—in the Pentagon, the White House, and even the Department of State—seemed to have come to the conclusion that there was a real danger of the Soviets unleashing, in the fairly near future, what would have been World War Three.

One of the most interesting subjects for historical inquiry would be, even today, the reasons why this conclusion became so current in Washington at that time. I opposed it; so did my colleague Charles Bohlen: both without success. I can only attribute it to the difficulty many Americans seemed to have in accepting the idea that there could be a political threat, and particularly one emanating from a strong military power, which was not also, and primarily, a military threat. Particularly powerful seems to have been the temptation, especially in military quarters, to leap to the conclusion that since the Soviet leaders of the Stalin period were antagonistic towards us, since they were heavily armed, and since they were seriously challenging our world leadership, therefore they were just like the Nazis of recent memory; therefore they wanted and intended to go to war against us; and therefore policy towards them must be in accordance with the model of what policy towards the Nazis ought to have been before the outbreak of hostilities in 1939. None of this was correct.

In any case, this change in American opinion did occur at the time I mentioned—in late 1949 and early 1950. And one of its first consequences was the growth of a strong feeling in the American military and political establishments that we could not leave Japan demilitarized—that, on the contrary, we must garrison it for an indefinite period to come, even if this meant the conclusion of a separate Japanese peace treaty, not agreed to by the Russians. This view was made manifest publicly in a number of ways in early 1950, at the same time that we greatly reduced our military presence in South Korea. And the immediate Russian reaction to all this took the form of permitting, if not encouraging, the North Koreans to attack South Korea with a view to extending communist control to the entire Korean peninsula. If Japan was to remain indefinitely a bastion of American military power, if there was to be no agreed peace settlement for Japan, and if Moscow was to have no look-in on the Japanese situation, then Moscow wanted, by way of compensation, to consolidate its military-political position in Korea, which we appeared not to care too much about in any case.

This was the origin of the Korean War, as I see it; and you know the rest. Three years and 54,000 American casualties later, the conflict was terminated, but it was terminated by a stalemate on the Korean peninsula much like what we had had before—simply with a much heavier American involvement. And there it has remained to this day.

Now, what I think we should note about this episode are the following points. First, we Americans had little interest in negotiating with the Russians a political settlement of the problems of that region, and particularly one which would have put an end to our military presence in Japan. And why did we have so little interest in this? Mainly, I suppose, because we had already made up our minds that Moscow was determined to launch a new world war. To resist this, we needed Japan as a military outpost. But also, Russia was already identified as the epitome of evil; and it wouldn't look good, from the domestic political standpoint, to be negotiating and compromising with evil.

The second thing I want to point out is that when, then, the Russians reacted as they did, by authorizing—or acquiescing in—the North Korean attack, we were never willing or even able to recognize the connection between what we had done in Japan and what the North Korean Communists were doing in Korea. On the contrary, when the North Korean attack came, the immediate conclusion in Washington was that this was indeed the first move in a Soviet program of worldwide military expansion, comparable to the Munich crisis of 1938 which was so often seen as the first Nazi move in the conquest of Europe. Again, both Bohlen and I challenged this interpretation; but we could make little headway against it. It was the military interpretation that prevailed.

Now, bearing all that in mind, let me turn to the other great involvement of this country in Far Eastern affairs in the postwar period, one that lasted twenty-five years instead of only three: the Vietnam War. I must assume here that all of you have some memories or some knowledge of that prolonged, expensive, unsuccessful, and in every way unfortunate effort on our part to defeat what we saw as the Vietnamese communists (they were really primarily nationalists) and to install some sort of anticommunist government in that country. This effort was obviously tragically misconceived. It is clearly recognizeable today as a tremendous blunder of American policy, and it raises two great historical questions to which we today ought to give that most careful attention. The first is how we got into the mess in the first place. And the second is why, since it was evident almost from the start that the effort could not be successful, we persisted in it for more than a decade.

In each case, the reasons were complex: I do not want to oversimplify a complicated situation. But I might just say this: Among the reasons for getting into this tangle in the first place, an important part was played by the belief in Washington that the Russians, as part of their design for world domination, were bent on the military-political conquest of Asia, and that the effort of the Vietnamese communists to establish their power in Southeast Asia was a part of this supposed "design."

Essential to this scenario we had created for ourselves was the belief that Ho Chi Minh and his followers were only puppets of the Russians, and that therefore a takeover by them in Vietnam would be equivalent to a Soviet conquest. There was general disbelief in Washington that these Vietnamese Marxists could be more strongly motivated by nationalistic impulses than by their Marxist ideological views.

Both these assumptions were wrong. The Soviet leadership had no preconceived design for world conquest. Its psychology was primarily defensive. Moscow had little, if anything, to do with Ho Chi Minh's efforts to take power in Vietnam at that time. We know today that Soviet connections with the communists in Southeast Asia were at that time actually distant and rudimentary. Ho Chi Minh was indeed primarily a nationalist who, despite his communist ideological rhetoric, would probably have been glad to keep a certain balance in his relations with the Communist world and with us, had we encouraged him to do so. Several of our best experts tried vainly to tell us this.

Let me expand a bit on this tendency of ours to insist on seeing as blind puppets of some other great power weaker or smaller factions or regimes whose relations with that great power are actually much more complicated and much less sinister than that. There seems to be a curious American tendency to search, at all times, for a single external center of evil, to which all our troubles can be attributed, rather than to recognize that there might be multiple sources of resistance to our purposes and undertakings, and that these sources might be relatively independent of each other.

Let me give examples. In the patriotic emotionalism that overcame our country during the First World War, the unfortunate German Kaiser came to be seen as the fountainhead of all that was bad and reprehensible in this world. And because the first thing the Russian communists did when they seized power in 1917 was to take Russia out of the war, and because this benefited the Germans, and was therefore disagreeable to us, the entire Russian Revolution had to be in some way attributed to the Kaiser. Many good people came to believe that Lenin and his associates were simply acting as German agents. And if we carry this inquiry down to the present day, we see the strong disinclination on the part of distinguished Americans to believe that the rulers of such countries as Nicaragua or Syria might be, despite their primitive Marxist utterances, in large measure independent political agents, acting primarily in their own interests as they see them, and not men deferring blindly to orders or ideological pressures from Moscow. Evil, in other words, must always be seen in many American eyes, in the singular. Virtue, on the other hand, may be graciously allowed to appear in the plural case, it being understood, of course, that we Americans always stand at the center of it.

But let me get back to the Vietnam episode and have a glance at the second of the great questions it raises: namely, why we continued this effort for nearly two decades when it was clear to each successive administration that the effort was a hopeless one.

Here, the answer is no less significant.

All this was happening on the heels of the triumph of the Chinese Communists in the Chinese civil war. And this development, let us remember, had been made the occasion for the most violent and reckless attacks on the Truman administration by a group of right-wing senators and others generally known as the China Lobby: the charge being that the Democrats, and particularly the Secretary of State, Mr. Dean Acheson, had, as the phrase then went, "lost China," and that they had done this under the influence of communist sympathizers in their official entourage who wanted the Communists to win.

Never could there have been greater nonsense than this. The United States government had never *had* China. Not having had China, it could scarcely have lost it. The basic condition making possible the Communist takeover in that country was the weakness and corruption of the Chiang Kai-shek regime, and the tendency of that regime to lean on us instead of pulling up its own socks. And not only was the charge in itself absurd, but the political attacks launched in its name against Messrs. Truman and Acheson were as vicious and irresponsible as any, I think, that American political history has to offer. These attacks were in fact closely connected with, and actually an early part of, the wave of anticommunist hysteria which was soon to become known as McCarthyism—an episode of our public life so disgraceful that one blushes today to think about it.

I have the impression that the emotional background of that particular hysteria still awaits its historical analysis. But what I want to point out here is simply that not only the Truman administration but its Republican successor as well were so intimidated by the violence of these attacks and by the extent of the response they evoked in Congress and in portions of our public opinion that they could never bring themselves to confront them head-on intellectually. The Truman administration, viewing them exclusively as partisan political attacks and ignoring their effect in distorting public opinion on foreign policy issues, tried to deflect them by professing some degree of sympathy for their premises and by appropriating to itself a certain amount of their rhetoric. The same was true of the Eisenhower administration that succeeded it, which even went so far as to sacrifice several of the best experts we had on Far Eastern matters, in the hopes of appeasing the authors of the attacks.

The results were appalling. Not only did these reckless vendettas inflict traumas that have affected the American political establishment down to the present day (I shall have more to say about that in the last of these lectures) but they seriously distorted the understanding of a great many Americans about foreign policy, implying as they did that our policy was always the decisive mover of events everywhere in the world; that in any country of the world, including China, we had it in our power to prevent the rise to positions of authority of people professing Marxist sympathies; and that therefore if a communist takeover nevertheless occurred somewhere, this was always attributable to the faint-heartedness or the remissness or the blindness or the lack of a suitable anticommunism on the part of the American administration then in office. Because of the failure of successive administrations to challenge head-on these outrageous imputations, those administrations repeatedly became the victims of them. And so it was in Vietnam. Not only did no administration feel that it could afford to be seen as unwilling to make the effort to oppose a communist takeover in Vietnam, but no administration, down to that of Mr. Nixon, having once engaged itself in such an effort and having been obliged to recognize that the effort was hopeless, dared to try to extract itself from the involvement at all, for fear of being pilloried by the silly charge that it had "lost Vietnam."

In the second of these lectures I shall deal more extensively with the general lessons that flow from the episodes I have been discussing here. I would only like to observe at this point that the failings we have been looking at this morning were primarily those of what we might call popular diplomacy as opposed to professional diplomacy. The problems presented by these episodes could seldom be reduced to simple choices among only two or three alternatives. Like most great problems of foreign affairs they usually involved a bewildering welter of conflicting considerations requiring, for their understanding, much historical background and much detailed study. Obviously, such complexities could not be fully taken account of in the unavoidable oversimplifications to which political orators, newspaper reporters, and television announcers are automatically reduced. It is no wonder that in the face of this particular helplessness, the crude stereotype should have prevailed over the sophisticated analysis, and that this stereotype should have lent itself, at every turn, to domestic political exploitation rather than to clarification of our international problems.

This situation constitutes in itself, I believe, a great national problem. It is to this problem that I hope to return, if only briefly in the second of these lectures.

II

AMERICAN DIPLOMACY AND THE MILITARY

✿

AS I POINTED out when I spoke here last week, the lectures I gave so many years ago at the University of Chicago were critical in nature: and so was the talk I gave here last week. I attempted to identify the relationship between challenge and response in American diplomacy. Where the response did not seem to measure up to the challenge, I tried to spot the weaknesses of analysis or concept that led to the failure. So critical was this exercise, that it occurred to me after delivering that last lecture that some of you must be asking: Did we ever do anything right?

If this is what you are thinking, I recognize that I am at fault for having provoked such a question. But the answer to the questions is, Of course we did. We did many things right. The Marshall Plan was a great act of statesmanship. The generally nonpunitive treatment of our defeated enemies in the wake of the two world wars stands to our credit. There were, I am sure, many cases of helpful economic aid programs. There were dozens of cases, too, where we intervened helpfully and generously in the case of earthquakes, floods, or famines elsewhere in the world. An example was the great famine relief program we conducted in Russia in 1920 and 1921. And I remember my pride, as American ambassador in Yugoslavia in 1963, over the speed and efficiency with which an American field hospital, sent by our army in Germany, moved down to help the victims of the Skopje earthquake.

Then, too, there were a great many stupid things we could have done but wisely refrained from doing; and for that as well, the respective American statesmen deserve high praise, although they seldom get it. So our record is far from being only one of failures. On balance, we have little to be ashamed about. The rest of the world can be thankful that if a great world power had to arise on this magnificent North American territory in the last three centuries (and this could not have been avoided), it was one as peaceably and generously minded as this one. The offenses we have offered to our world environment since the establishment of our independence have been ones arising as a rule not from any desire on our part to bring injury to others or to establish power over them, but from our attempts to strike noble postures and to impress ourselves. But just as it does the human individual more good to reflect upon his failings than upon his virtues, so, too, I think the national society has more to learn from its failures than from its successes. The contemplation of the failures induces humility—and that is something we Americans could well use more of. The contemplation of the successes leads only too easily to the pride that goes before a fall. So I shall continue, appealing to your patience, to talk about one or two further places where our thinking was at fault and where we made mistakes.

Looking back over what has already been said, I see that I have talked, both at Chicago and here, mostly about our policies with relation to the non-European world. But there was a great difference between the episodes I discussed back in 1950—those before the Second World War—and the ones I mentioned here last week. Although jingoism and a yearning for dramatic military exploits played a part in the case of the Spanish-American War, most of the faults to which I drew attention in the Chicago lectures were of the sort I just mentioned: the faults of a certain moralistic and legalistic posturing on our part—a desire to appear, particularly to ourselves, as more wise and more noble than we really were. In the case of Korea and Vietnam, on the other hand, something much more serious was involved: namely, the impression we had that we were confronted, for the first time since the birth of this republic, with a great, terrible, remorseless enemy, dedicated to our undoing, and holding in his hands the wherewithal to do us immense damage, even right here at home. This brought out fears, resentments, reactions, over-reactions, even temptations, on our part, in comparison with which our rather childish posturings and pretensions of earlier decades look innocent and naive.

And this brings me, of course, to the great and very real challenge of this post–World War Two period—a challenge consisting of the fact that when that war came to an end all but two of the traditional great powers of the modern age had fallen into a secondary military status—the two being the Soviet Union and the United States. And whereas these two powers had previously been widely separated from each other in a military sense by the geographic interposition of other great powers, the outcome of the Second World War eliminated this separation and placed their respective military forces in close proximity to each other in the center of Europe and in the northern Pacific. There was now nothing between them, as there had been in earlier decades, to absorb the impact of any serious political differences they might have. To this was added the unprecedented, and immensely disorienting, factor of the introduction into national arsenals of nuclear weaponry which, together with its delivery systems, made each of these so-called superpowers capable of reaching the homeland of the other and of inflicting upon it damages of an unpredictable but obviously horrendous order, so that each of these two powers became in effect the hostage of the other. The challenge this offered to American statesmanship was, then, How to respond to this utterly new and unheard of danger, for which history had no precedent—either in our own experience or in that of any other country.

I think it not surprising, in the circumstances, that mistakes were made. They were made, of course, not just on our side but on the Soviet side as well. The challenge was no less unusual, no less bewildering, for the Russians than it was for ourselves. And in dwelling, as I propose briefly to do, on our own mistakes, I would not wish you to think that I am oblivious to those made by people in Moscow. I would also not wish it to be thought that I considered that our response had consisted of nothing *but* mistakes. Here, too, no doubt, many necessary, well-pondered, and constructive things were done.

Still it is my belief that there *were* mistakes, and great far-reaching ones at that. And since certain of these mistakes seem to me to distort and bedevil our policy even down to the present day, to the great danger of ourselves and the rest of the world, I see no choice but to mention them.

One category of these mistakes consists of the ones I pointed to in the first of these lectures. These were the mistakes involved in attributing to the Soviet leadership aims and intentions it did not really have: in jumping to the conclusion that the Soviet leaders were just like Hitler and his associates, that they were animated by the same lusts for military conquest, that they had the same sort of timetables for external military aggression, and that they could be met and dealt with effectively only in the same way that Hitler had to be met and dealt with.

This view was given sustenance by the fact that at the end of the Second World War the Russians did not demobilize their armed forces to anything resembling the degree we did. They left a ground force establishment in eastern and central Europe far greater than anything that confronted them on the western side. They frightened everybody by behaving with great ruthlessness and brutality towards the peoples of the eastern and central European countries they occupied. They were wily and secretive in their dealings with us; and it was clear that they hoped, by various devices of political influence and authority, to extend their dominant influence, if not their direct power, as far as they could into Western Europe—and this at the expense of the freedoms of the Western European peoples themselves. The period I am speaking about was, after all, still the Stalin era.

All these things were evidence, indeed, of no friendly feelings towards ourselves on the part of the men in the Kremlin. They were evidence that we and the Western Europeans had on our hands a great and serious competitor for influence, and indeed for power, over the European continent and other parts of the world. But they were not proof that the Russians wanted another war. They were not proof that it was by the launching of their armed forces on some all-out attack against Western Europe or Japan that that the Soviet leaders intended to extend their influence. Yet these were the conclusions we jumped to. The consequences have been far-reaching.

The second of our great postwar mistakes had to do with our embracing the nuclear weapon as the mainstay of our military posture, and the faith we placed in it to assure our military and political ascendancy in this postwar era. We made the primitive error of supposing that the effectiveness of a weapon was directly proportionate to its destructiveness—destructiveness not just against an enemy's armed forces but against its population and its civilian economy as well. We forgot that the aim of war is, or should be, to gain one's points with the minimum, not the maximum, of general destruction, and that a proper weapon must be not only destructive but discriminating. Above all, we neglected to consider the strong evidence that the nuclear weapon could not be, in the long run, other than a suicidal one, partly because of its very destructiveness, together with the virtual certainty that others would develop it, but also because of its probable environmental effects. And by this commitment to a weapon that was both suicidal and unsuitable to any rational military purpose we incurred, in my opinion, a heavy share of the blame for leading large parts of the international community into the most dangerous and fateful weapons race the world has ever known.

It is from these two great mistakes that there has flowed, as I see it, that extreme militarization not only of our thought but of our lives that has become the mark of this postwar age. And this is a militarization that has had profound effects not just on our foreign policies but also on our own society. It has led to what I and many others have come to see as a serious distortion of our national economy. We have been obliged to habituate ourselves to the expenditure annually of a great portion of our national income on the production and export of armaments, and the maintenance of a vast armed force establishment —purposes that add nothing to the real productive capacity of our economy, and only deprive us every year of tens of billions of dollars that might otherwise go into productive investment. And this habit has now risen to the status of what I have ventured to call a genuine national addiction. We could not now break ourselves of this habit without the most serious of withdrawal symptoms. Millions of people, in addition to those other millions that are in uniform, have become accustomed to deriving their livelihood from the military-industrial complex. Thousands of firms have become dependent on it, not to mention labor unions and communities. It is the main source of our highly destabilizing budgetary deficit. An elaborate and most unhealthy bond has been created between those who manufacture and sell the armaments and those in Washington who buy them. We have, in other words, created immense vested interests in the maintenance of a huge armed establishment in time of peace and in the export of great quantities of arms to other peoples—great vested interests, in other worlds, in the cold war. We have made ourselves dependent on this invidious national practice—so much so that it may fairly be said that if we did not have the Russians, and their alleged iniquities, to serve as a rationalization for it, we would have to invent some adversary to take their place.

The problem is made worse by the unnecessary wastefulness of this entire exercise, by the interservice rivalries that cause so much duplication of effort, by the double standard we apply to costs and results as between the military economy and the civilian one, by the lack of any coherent relationship between the criteria our Congress applies to military expenditures and those it applies to nonmilitary ones. It sometimes seems to me that those of us not involved in this great military-industrial enterprise are in danger of becoming, in the figurative sense, a nation of camp followers, like the pathetic stragglers who trailed along behind the European armies of earlier centuries in the hopes of picking up remnants from the relative abundance of the military resources of food and clothing.

When this phenomenon distorts our lives internally, this reacts, again, adversely on our foreign policy. So great a military economy requires constant justification, and this—intensified by the fierce competition of the three principal armed services for congressional appropriations—leads to an almost automatic and systematic over-representation of the military potential of the supposed adversary, thereby heightening the suspicion of that adversary, and the fear and antagonism addressed to him, in our population. The figures on supposed Soviet military expenditures put out in recent years from certain quarters within our government have been among the most shamelessly tendentious and misleading statistical manipulations I can recall seeing. And the worst feature of all this is that it confuses and obscures the real dimensions of the external political challenge. It becomes impossible to know how much of our behavior is a justifiable response to the problem the Soviet Union presents for us, and how much is the product of our own commitment to our military-industrial addiction.

I say all these things simply to make the point that the great militarization of our view of the Cold War that has grown upon us increasingly over the years is not only an external danger for this country but an internal one as well, in the form of a highly pernicious habit to which great parts of our society are almost hopelessly committed. And much of this is traceable, once again, back to those two great faults of analysis to which I have just drawn attention: The one involving the nature of Soviet expansionist policies and intentions; the other concerning our failure to spot the terrible blind alley into which we would bring ourselves, and much of the rest of the world, when we consigned the leading role in our military policy to the nuclear weapon and the other weapons of mass destruction.

Let me try, then, to sum up the main conclusions to which I am carried by the observations I have put before you here, and by the earlier ones brought forward in the Chicago lectures.

We have seen a wide variety of the faults of American diplomacy, as they have revealed themselves over the entire span of the twentieth century. Up to the Second World War they were largely the faults of a young and somewhat naive people, overtaken by the heady and disorienting forces of modern nationalism, coupled with the unsettling consciousness of our own growing strength, which was rapidly elevating us into the ranks of the major powers. We were affected, in those years, by something of the relatively innocent erraticism of the adolescent who is becoming aware of his own strength and would like to use it, but lacks the maturity to know how best to do so.

Since this last great war a wholly different situation has come into being. We have been put, as a nation, to entirely different tests— obliged to deal with a wholly different order of demands, some of them involving a greater responsibility than any statesmen anywhere have ever faced.

Now sometimes we have responded, I think, as well as any country could or would have responded to the various challenges implicit in these situations; but in other instances, as I hope these lectures have shown, we have not. And if I look at the cases where we have not, and run over the apparent reasons for our failures, I think I see two factors which, taken together, give us the clue to the greatest of our difficulties.

The instances where we have fallen down most frequently and most seriously seem all to have been ones in which military affairs were involved. Sometimes the fault lay in our analysis of situations elsewhere in the world. We tend to overemphasize military factors at the expense of political ones, and in consequence, overmilitarize our responses. Sometimes, as in the cases of the two world wars, it has been a question of the use to be made of our own military potential—how and when to employ it, and then, when employed, how to relate it to the remainder of our national life. Sometimes, finally, as in the case of the nuclear weapon, the problem has been in our ability or inability to think through the possible uses of modern weaponry, and, indeed, the uses of war itself as between great industrial nations in this modern age. But in each case it is the military factor that has tripped us up.

When you stop to think about it, this is not surprising. We are a nation which has no traditional concepts of military strategy or of the place of military power in the structure of our national life. Except for our own Civil War, which was quite a different thing and was fought for a different purpose, our involvements with the use of armed force in the modern age have occurred primarily in the confusing and to some extent misleading experiences of the two world wars of the century. Both these wars ended in unconditional surrender, encouraging us in the view that the purpose of war was not to bring about a mutually advantageous compromise with an external adversary seen as totally evil and inhuman, but to destroy completely the power and the will of that adversary. In both those wars, but particularly the second, we departed increasingly from the principle, embodied in the earlier rules of warfare, that war should be waged only against the armed forces of an enemy, not against the helpless civilian population. And it was by our wholehearted acceptance of the practice of waging war against civilians as well as against soldiers, and especially by our commitment to the so-called area bombings of World War II, that we were led into the terrible bewilderments we are confronting today. We are now finally being brought to recognize that to follow that practice to its logical conclusion is to destroy ourselves and probably civilization itself. We have, in other words, worked ourselves into a blind alley; and now, as we try to retreat from this dreadful trap, it is becoming apparent to us that we have no workable alternative theory of the uses of armed force to fall back on. Both of these errors—the commitment to unconditional surrender and the commitment to massive civilian destruction—have led us seriously astray.

And it is not surprising that we should have trouble relating military matters to the internal problems of our society. We have never had the tradition of maintaining standing armies in peacetime. We have never learned how to fit that practice in with the other habits and needs of our society in point of education, civic training, and man-power use. Even worse than that, we have not been able to find any very rational way to relate to the other processes of our society the industrial and financial effort required to maintain a great armed forces establishment in what is nominally a time of peace.

No wonder, in the face of all this confusion, that our greatest mistakes in national policy seem to occur where the military factor is most prominently involved.

But I wonder whether this confusion is not compounded by certain deeply ingrained features of our political system. I am thinking first of all about what I might call the domestic political selfconsciousness of the American statesman. By this I mean his tendency, when speaking or acting on matters of foreign policy, to be more concerned for the domestic political effects of what he is saying or doing than about their actual effects on our relations with other countries. In the light of this tendency, a given statement or action will be rated as a triumph in Washington if it is applauded at home in those particular domestic circles at which it is aimed, even if it is quite ineffective or even self-defeating in its external effects. When this is carried to extremes, American diplomacy tends to degenerate into a series of postures struck before the American political audience, with only secondary consideration being given to the impacts of these postures on our relations with other countries.

This situation is not new. We have only to recall Tocqueville's words, written 150 years ago, to the effect that "it is in the nature of democracies to have, for the most part, the most confused or erroneous ideas on external affairs, and to decide questions of foreign policy on purely domestic considerations." Nor is this, in essence, unnatural. Every statesman everywhere has to give *some* heed to domestic opinion in the conduct of his diplomacy. But the tendency seems to be carried to greater extremes here than elsewhere. This may be partly explained by the nature of the constituency to which the American statesman appeals. In the European parliamentary systems, the constituency is normally the parliament—because the ministry can fall from office if it loses parliamentary support. In our country, unhappily, the constituencies are more likely to consist of particularly aggressive and vociferous minorities or lobbies. These, for some curious reason, seem more often than not to be on the militaristic and chauvinistic side, either because there is some particular nation or ethnic group abroad which they want our government to support, militarily or otherwise, or because they like to wrap themselves in the national emblem and beat the jingoist bell as a means of furthering their partisan purposes. American administrations seem to be particularly vulnerable, as we saw in the first of these lectures, to just this sort of intimidation, presumably because they do not want to be placed on the defensive by being charged with lack of patriotism. And the effects of this are ones we have had occasion to note, both in connection with our policies in third world areas, such as Vietnam or Lebanon, and in connection with the problems of arms control and the relations among the great military powers.

If there is any substance to what I have just been saying, then this is simply further evidence for the fact, to which many wise observers beside Tocqueville have drawn attention, that our political system is in many ways poorly designed for the conduct of the foreign policies of a great power aspiring to world leadership. I, in any case, believe this to be true, and I consider that the trend of events in these recent years has revealed deficiencies in this system which even Tocqueville could not foresee.

What are we going to do about it? It would be naive of us to expect, or even to hope, that these features of our governmental system are going to be corrected within our time. To try to correct them abruptly might well do more harm than good. In many respects, they represent the reverse side of the great coin of the liberties we so dearly cherish. And in this sense I see no reason why we should be ashamed of them. If this—our political system with all its faults—is the only way that a great mass of people such as our own, stretching from Florida to Alaska and from Maine to Hawaii and embracing individuals of the most diverse ethnic and cultural origins—if this is the only way such a mass of people can be governed without the sacrifice of their liberties —then so be it; and let us be thankful that such a possibility exists at all, even if it is not a perfect one.

But the one thing we *can* do, in the face of this situation, is to take realistic account of this unsuitability of our political system for the conduct of an ambitious and far-reaching foreign policy, and to bear these limitations in mind when we decide which involvements and responsibilities it is wise for us to accept and which would be better rejected. Obviously, a number of the responsibilities we have already accepted, including some of the very greatest ones—NATO and our obligations to Japan, for example—represent solemn commitments of which we cannot divest ourselves at any early date. There is nothing for us to do but to meet these commitments as best we can, recognizing that the peace and safety not just of our country but of much of the rest of the world as well depends on the way we meet them, and trying to place them, wherever we can, above the partisan political interests that every American administration is bound to have. But when it comes to the acceptance of new responsibilities, let us, at long last, try to bear in mind the limits of our national capabilities and the price we are obliged to pay for our liberties. Let us recognize that there are problems in this world that we will not be able to solve, depths into which it will not be useful or effective for us to plunge, dilemmas in other regions of the globe that will have to find their solution without our involvement.

This is not a plea for a total isolationism, such as our grandfathers and great-grandfathers cultivated. It is only a request, if I may put it that way, for a greater humility in our national outlook, for a more realistic recognition of our limitations as a body politic, and for a greater restraint than we have shown in recent decades in involving ourselves in complex situations far from our shores. And it is a plea that we bear in mind that in the interaction of peoples, just as in the interactions of individuals, the power of example is far greater than the power of precept, and that the example offered to the world at this moment by the United States of America is far from being what it could be and ought to be. Let us present to the world outside our borders the face of a country that has learned to cope with crime and poverty and corruption, with drugs and pornography. Let us prove ourselves capable of taking the great revolution in electronic communication in which we are all today embraced and turning it to the intellectual and spiritual elevation of our people in place of the enervation and debilitation and abuse of the intellect that the TV set now so often inflicts upon them. Let us do these things, and others like them, and we will not need 27,000 nuclear warheads and a military budget of over $250 billion to make the influence of America felt in the world beyond our borders.

It is on that note that I would like to end these lectures, thanking you for the patience with which you have endured them, and absolving you of further involvement with the views of one elderly individual on so many highly complex subjects.

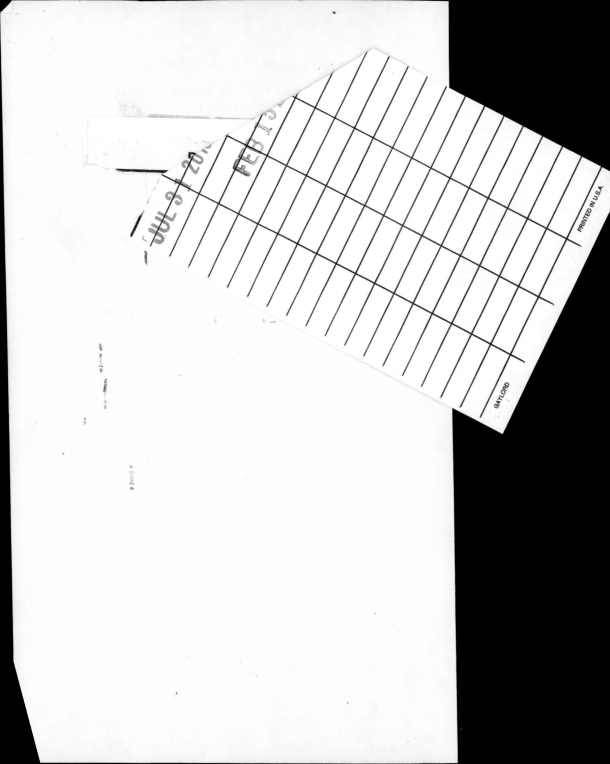